Napa
VALLEY

PICTURE PERFECT

PRODUCED IN COOPERATION WITH

THE NAPA CHAMBER OF COMMERCE

Napa VALLEY

PICTURE PERFECT

Produced in partnership with the
Napa Chamber of Commerce
Mark Richmond, President
1556 First Street
P.O. Box 636
Napa, CA 94559-06736

By Tony Kilgallin
Corporate Profiles by Christine Bettencourt
and Amy Taramasso
Featuring the photography of Nanci Kerby
Staff for *Napa Valley: Picture Perfect*
Publisher's Sales Associate: Marlene Berg
Executive Editor: James E. Turner
Senior Editor: Mary Shaw Hughes
Managing Editors: Amy Newell and Linda Pegram
Profile Editor: Mary Catherine Richardson
Design Director: Scott Phillips
Designer: Matt Johnson
Photo Editors: Matt Johnson and Amy Newell
Production Manager: Jarrod Stiff
Editorial Assistant: Amanda J. Burbank
Contract Manager: Christi Stevens
Sales Coordinator: Annette R. Lozier
Accounting Services: Sara Ann Turner
Printing Production: Gary G. Pulliam/DC Graphics
Pre-press and Separations: Artcraft Graphic Productions

C C I

Community Communications, Inc.
Montgomery, Alabama

James E. Turner, *Chairman of the Board*
Ronald P. Beers, *President*
Daniel S. Chambliss, *Vice President*

Table of Contents

Part One

CHAPTER ONE:
THE PRIDE OF CALIFORNIA, 14

Once known as Talahalusi, meaning "Beautiful Land," the
Napa Valley was first inhabited by Native Americans. Then
in 1831, George Yount became the region's first white
inhabitant, beginning a wave of settlement that forever
changed the face of the valley. These settlers' stories of
challenge, triumph, and disappointment provide a lasting
testament to their determination to survive—and succeed.

CHAPTER TWO:
VITICULTURE & VINTNERS, 28

Napa's vineyards and wineries have earned worldwide
fame, and a tour of "Wine Country" will show many
reasons why. The area's vineyards are steeped in both history
and beauty. This journey to a variety of wineries and
wine-growing regions offers an enticing taste of
Napa Valley enchantment.

CHAPTER THREE:
A CLUSTER OF CHOICES, 44

The Valley offers a variety of cultural and recreational
attractions, from Calistoga's famous hot springs to the
Culinary Institute of America to the di Rosa Preserve of
Art and Nature. Take a trip along Napa's 30-mile-long
"land-ladder" and see top-notch sites.

CHAPTER FOUR:
GRAPE EXPECTATIONS, 60

While looking ahead to the future, Napa residents also are
preserving their past. Restoration, renovation, and
revitalization are bringing about a renaissance in
downtown Napa.

Part Two 2

All photographs in Part 1 by Nanci Kerby.
Additional photographs by Nanci Kerby are on pages 74, 76,
91, 92, 99, 100, 114, 119, 120, 126, 131, and 133.

Foreword

"The beginning of vine-planting is like the beginning of mining for precious metals," wrote Robert Louis Stevenson in 1880. Instead of producing ore, he said, the precious vineyards "yield inimitable fragrance and soft fire…"

The earth of the Napa Valley has truly yielded a bounty of riches: gold, silver, grapes, prunes, mustard, abundant natural beauty, and a quality of life envied around the world. A major motion picture captured Napa's beauty in 1940, and its fame has grown ever since. The county has retained its pastoral appearance through residents' abiding commitment to the agricultural preserve.

Valley residents have worked to produce not only world-class wines but also communities of which they are justifiably proud. Advances, often sponsored by the Napa Chamber of Commerce, include a county airport, downtown revitalization, countywide flood control, corporate parks, and world-class resorts.

A renaissance of the city of Napa has begun to unfold, with the establishment of the American Center for Wine, Food and the Arts on the east side of First Street and the Factory Outlet Stores on the west. As a national model, the flood-control project promises a riverfront that will charm and entertain visitors and residents alike. This expansion also extends to new high-tech industry and warehousing in south Napa County, which will generate new capital to ensure a vital economy.

As we move forward in the 21st century, the Napa Chamber of Commerce—now 111 years old—pledges to continue its work in the community, celebrating the Century of Commitment. Working cooperatively with other valley chambers, the Napa Chamber focuses on meeting today's challenges. Special programs such as Leadership Napa Valley, El Mercado, the Economic Summit, and the Business Showcase contribute to a robust economy and a commitment to serve others.

We invite you to contemplate the delights of the Napa Valley, where, as Stevenson wrote, "…the stirring sunlight and the growing vines, and the vats and bottles in the cavern, made a pleasant music for the mind."

Ed Shenk, President, 1999   Mark Richmond, President, 2000
Napa Chamber of Commerce   Napa Chamber of Commerce

Preface

On Tuesday, December 20, 1859, the author-statesman Richard Henry Dana recorded in his memoir *A Voyage Round the World* that "Napa Valley is the pride of California." A century later, novelist Arthur Hailey sent this succinctly seductive telegram to his wife, Sheila:

> *Napa Valley California is a few feet this side of paradise. It is everything we have dreamed about and love. Climate superb. Spring in February. All year outdoor country living combined with city closeness. Local schools excellent. San Francisco one hour drive. Today I bought half acre in Meadowood development on glorious hillside overlooking valley and mountains… begin planning our future home. Love, Arthur*

Napa Valley: Picture Perfect is a full-scale enlargement of the visions epitomized by Dana and Hailey. As an acronym, NAPA stands for the quiet synergy of Nature's sun and soils with the skills and sweat of Artists. P includes the Preservation of viticulture, the Patience for slow growth, and the Philosophy of Prosperity via long-range Perspectives. Part Mayberry, part Brigadoon, from seed to grape, from promise to performance, Napa Valley represents enterprising Actions grown from Aspirations and Ambitions. It's a grape place to live and love.

Part One

CHAPTER 1

The Pride of California

The home known today as Tusitala began as a small, two-story ranch house built in the 1840s. Thomas and Elizabeth Rutherford, who married in 1864, expanded the home to its present size. The Ritchie family, who now own the property, have renamed it Tusitala— Samoan for "storyteller"—in honor of Robert Louis Stevenson. The famous writer came to Napa Valley in 1880, and the climate helped him overcome a bout of tuberculosis.

Every settler seeks a second chance, whatever the century, wherever the land. The human spirit strives to regain paradise lost, to find a soil that matches his or her soul. Everything that makes the Napa Valley unique stems from its geography and geology. Its bounty germinates from the soil. The fascinating history of Napa is perhaps best understood from listening to the stories of the individuals who wrote their letters from the soil and shared their own perspectives of time and place.

The Big Picture

Napa County was one of California's original 27 counties established shortly after the state was admitted to the Union in 1850. Its area is 758 square miles or 500,000 acres, bordered by the Mayacamas Mountains to the west and the parallel Vaca Range to the east. These mountains shield the Valley in winter from cold Pacific Ocean winds 30 miles westward, while in summertime, they protect the Valley from the intense interior heat of central California. Its highest point is Mt. St. Helena, towering 4,334 feet. Its largest body of water, Lake Berryessa, is 21 miles long.

Napa County has been designated an agricultural land preserve, and the majority of the county's resources are dedicated to wine grape production. There are 34,000 acres of grapes and 240 wineries within the 35-mile long Napa Valley.

At its southern end, the Valley is about 8 miles wide, slowly tapering to the north where Mt. St. Helena becomes its boundary. The Valley is drained by the Napa River, north to south. Sixteen navigable miles below Napa City, the river empties into San Pablo Bay, part of San Francisco Bay. Napa City is 50 miles north of San Francisco.

Prehistory

Once known as *Talahalusi*, meaning "Beautiful Land," the Napa Valley is one of California's oldest inhabited areas. Archaeological surveys indicate 10,000 years of uninterrupted habitation.

"It was a paradise—a cultivated paradise where one had only to extend one's hand to eat. A place rich in beauty, water, and food," states the oral history of Native American Elder Jim Big Bear King.

Native Americans lived peacefully in pole houses, using clamshell beads and magnesite cylinders for money and jewelry. They processed obsidian into shafts, spears, and arrowheads for hunting and export. Acorns, perennial grasses, wild berries, freshwater shellfish, salmon, fowl, and game were their diet.

When George Yount, Napa Valley's first white settler, visited in 1831, he estimated 3,000 to 5,000 Indians living in the Valley. By 1855, only 500 remained.

The Caymus Grant

The first tract of land ever granted by the Mexican government to parties in what is now known as Napa County, was ceded to George Yount. He arrived when the whole domain lay in its virginity—before the foot of a white man had ever trod upon it—his was the first. The Caymus Grant lies in the very heart of Napa Valley, just east of the present village of Yountville.

How Yount acquired the grant is an engaging tale.

A Story Is Told

In 1835, the Mexican Commandante General Vallejo, age 28, was constructing a large home in Sonoma County, when George Yount, age 42, appeared on the scene looking for work. "What can you do?" demanded Vallejo.

"Many things," said Yount.

Vallejo replied, "I do not want you to do many things; what one thing can you do that no one else does here?"

"I have seen no shingles in California; your new house yonder is about ready for them. I can make shingles," remarked Yount.

Somewhat confused, Vallejo stammered, "What are tzin-tzin…how do you call them…tzingals?"

Yount explained and took him through the entire process: barking the felled redwood, crosscutting it into blocks 18 inches long, splitting and shaving—all with the simple tools of a frontiersman.

"Very well," replied Vallejo, who had followed him attentively, though half incredulously, "You shall make me some tzingals and roof my house."

The work was done, and the general was highly pleased; he had a "tzingaled" house—the first in both upper and lower California—and he was very proud of it.

"How shall I pay you?" inquired Vallejo.

"I would like some land in the Napa Valley, and a few heifers so that I might start a herd," replied the modest Yount.

Vallejo asked, "How much land?"

"Half a league," responded Yount.

But Vallejo objected. "You can't have half a league; we don't give half-leagues here, with 500 miles on our north and 1,000 on our east, unoccupied. You can have four leagues."

"I will take a league," said Yount, no doubt considering the care and cost of tending so large a tract.

But Vallejo would not hear of it.

"You can have two leagues and nothing less," he replied. And so the matter ended, with the shake-splitter acquiring 20 square miles, or 11,814.52 acres of virgin territory in the Napa Valley.

In 1838, George Yount planted the first grapes in Napa County, creating a vineyard no larger than a quarter-acre between his adobe home and the Napa River. Over 150 years later, the property has grown to become a 350-acre vineyard under the able stewardship of the Pelissa family. He also built the first log house, a Kentucky blockhouse erected on the Pacific coast, and the first chimney in California.

In 1858, Charles Krug produced the first modern wine in the Napa Valley. Viticulture as an industry had begun.

The Old Bale Mill, built by Dr. Edward Turner Bale in 1846, has changed little in more than a century. The mill, which ground grist and flour, served Napa Valley residents until 1879.

Napa Valley mineral water, touted for its health benefits, was sold in colorful bottles in the 1850s. The bottles are on display at the Napa Valley Museum in Yountville.

The Sentencing of Sergeant Cayetano Juarez

Faced with the probable desertion of all his unpaid soldiers, General Vallejo issued an ultimatum that deserters would be shot. The only one who tried to defect was captured, court-martialed, and sentenced to death. The only circumstance in his favor was that he was the troop's sole bachelor. Every female in the Mission prayed for Don Cayetano's release and petitioned en masse for a pardon.

In their presence, General Vallejo sentenced the 32-year-old prisoner: "Don Cayetano, at the request of these good women, I am giving you your life. You can never again be a soldier, but that need not prevent you from being a good man. You must marry, and I will give you an ample grant of land. Then you can help us civilize this fine country."

Thus, the Tulucay Rancho containing 8,865.58 acres was granted to Cayetano Juarez on October 26, 1841. Today, this land grant comprises the southeast quadrant of Napa City.

Bale's Mill

The "Old Bale Mill" stands almost as it was built by Dr. Edward Turner Bale in 1846. Florentine Ironworker and orchardist Erwin Kellogg, of Batavia, New York, who had crossed the plains with his wife and three children in a wagon train, did the iron work on Bale's mill. In return, Kellogg received 600 acres of the Bale Rancho. At work one evening, he counted 156 deer drinking at a mountain stream.

except in England. Great fields, level, rich, no undergrowth, fair sprinkling of large trees, and distances so great that the men are ploughing by flagstaffs, as a pilot would steer his ship. Peculiarity of valley is that it is enclosed by high hills, river wandering through it, lands nearly level, and small hills, green to top, dotted over the valley, which one can easily ride round or over—rising like artificial mounds…breakfasted by open door, few remaining strawberries on vines, grapes still on vines, and fresh flowers in bloom. The creeping vines over the veranda are in luxuriant bloom. Best of weather, wood fires and open doors. This is California winter."

Until 1879, the mill ground grist and flour for the inhabitants of the Upper Napa Valley. Bale's daughter, Caroline, married Charles Krug, and upon the land she received, they planted grapes. In 1858, Krug produced the first modern wine in the Napa Valley. Viticulture as an industry had begun.

A Town Is Born

In 1848, the town of Napa was founded by Nathan Coombs, a successful young pioneer and farm owner. In 1845, Coombs was rewarded for his labor with a parcel of land called Entre Napa Rancho. He gave this land to establish the town of Napa.

The survey map, dated 1847, bears this notation: "This place is situated at the head of navigation on Nappa Creek in the most fertile and desirable valley in California. Its soil is better adapted to cultivation of fruit, vines, grains, [and] vegetables than any other portion of this delightful country."

Pluck & Luck

William Imrie (1828-1921) was an exemplary settler of the Napa Valley. His Scottish family emigrated to Delaware County, New York, in 1830. Shipwrecked while sailing to California in the spring of 1853, Imrie nevertheless made his way from San Francisco to the gold mines of Placerville to Napa in the fall of this same year. For the next eight years, he worked as a ranch foreman for Nathan Coombs, the founder of Napa City. Imrie saved his money and bought a 500-acre ranch, Imrieville, in 1861. He sold this land in 1869, and the following year, he purchased a 243-acre estate three miles northeast of Napa, bordering on Napa Creek. He married in 1867, bringing his wife from the East. They produced ten children— seven boys and three girls. Stewarded by a direct descendant, the farm is a rich vineyard today.

California Winter

An excerpt from Richard Henry Dana's
A Voyage Round the World (1859)

"Napa Valley is the pride of California… Took coach for Napa City which reached at noon. Ride up Napa Valley is beautiful. Never saw so much land under the plough in the same space,

The Calistoga of Sarafornia

In 1859, Samuel Brannan purchased one square mile of land at Calistoga, including the famous Hot Springs. Brannan, California's first millionaire, spent his fortune in an attempt to make Calistoga the Saratoga of the Pacific. Spearheaded by Brannan, the Napa Railroad Company worked from 1864 to 1868 to connect the Napa Valley from south to north, Soscol to Napa City to Oakville, then on to Rutherford, St. Helena, and his own Calistoga. In October 1868, he used the railroad to bring over 3,000 guests from San Francisco to Sam Brannan's Hot Springs Resort! A Renaissance man, Brannan was the person who announced California's gold rush to the world, and he was California's first printer, banker, and promoter.

Either Ore

In 1861, John Newman discovered veins of cinnabar in Napa. Cinnabar is the principal ore used in the production of mercury. The Oat Hill Mine became one of the most productive cinnabar mines in the Calistoga area—and all on account of a dead dove. The hunter, William Paul Cook, spotted the rich ore deposit while trying to locate a bird he had just shot.

During that time, Chinese labor was used extensively in all the mines and most of the wine caves. The long underground tunnels at the Beringer Winery are proof of this labor. Less known is that in 1887, during the grape harvest, it rained so hard that wagons were unable to drive into the vineyards to load the grapes. The Chinese workers waded barefoot through the mud and carried out the grapes by hand.

All the News

Three of the oldest newspapers—the daily *Napa Valley Register* (started in 1863), the weekly *St. Helena Star* (1874), and the *Calistogan* (1877), still serve their communities.

Among other newspaper ventures in the Napa Valley, primarily based and circulated in the city of Napa, were the *Napa County Reporter* (1856), the *Napa Advertiser* (1866), the *Napa Evening Reporter* (1866), the *Pacific Echo* (1863), the *Reflector* (1896), the *Napa Semi-Weekly Sun* (1858), the *Gold Dollar* (1878), the *Napa Independent* (1909), and the *Napa Journal* (1890).

How the Rutherford Ranch Became Tusitala

In the late 1840s, a small, two-story wooden ranch house was erected on the north portion of the Rancho Caymus. Used in the home's construction were redwood lumber and shingles from the Yount sawmill. In 1864, George Yount gave his granddaughter Elizabeth 2,200 acres of the Rancho Caymus as a wedding present when she married Thomas Rutherford of San Francisco. It became the Rutherford Ranch and included the original ranch house.

The Rutherfords then expanded the house following the dimensions of George Yount's adobe structure in Yountville—20 feet wide by 110 feet long and two stories high. However, their home was built of redwood planks instead of adobe. Although it was constructed entirely of wood, the house featured the popular Monterey architectural style, with a veranda along its entire length on one side, and a more formal front on the other side with three small portico entrances.

The house was moved in 1987, and the original ranch house, which had been the south end, is now the north end. The home's new owners, the Ritchies, renovated the house and restored it to a single-family home, adding a raised foundation, large decks, and a screened-in porch. The building was found to be entirely constructed of heavy redwood planks and square nails. The Ritchies not only moved the house, but also its hand-cut basement stones, bricks, and even shrubs. The gateposts, chimney, and driveway are made from the stones. The property was renamed "Tusitala" (Samoan for storyteller) in memory of Robert Louis Stevenson.

"Nappa" Leather

In 1869, Sawyer's Tannery was begun by F.A. Sawyer with one co-worker, and they dyed sheepskins and deerskins. In 1875, a new foreman discovered an improved method for preparing sheepskins for glove leather. A patent was secured, and, by 1880, 1,200 sheepskins and 200 deerskins were being processed daily. By 1881, the firm showed its spirit of liberality by increasing the men's wages 14 percent, ranging from 75 cents a day for beginning boys to $2.75 a day for foremen.

Silverado Squatters

In June and July of 1880, the Robert Louis Stevensons honeymooned at the abandoned Silverado Mine, north of Calistoga. Suffering from tuberculosis, Stevenson hoped that the dry climate would cure him. His stay, high on the shoulder of Mt. St. Helena, arrested the spread of his disease, allowing him 14 more years of productivity. *The Silverado Squatters* (1883) is a highly descriptive, contemporary chronicle of the Upper Napa Valley.

Toward a Century of Commitment

On September 30, 1889, 80 community leaders gathered at the county courthouse and united as one body to further the public interest of Napa City and Napa County. They named their organization the Napa Improvement Society. In 1896, the organization was renamed Napa Board of Trade, reflecting the community's commercial ambitions. Indeed, according to the county assessor, on July 16, 1890, the total value of all property in Napa County was $11,131,815. Of this amount, $9,264,180 reflected the total value of real estate and improvements.

January 1904 saw the Board of Trade redefining itself as the Napa Chamber of Commerce. The by-laws declared that any person of good moral character could become a member with no joining fee, but with monthly dues of 50 cents upon approval. A member could serve on any of six standing committees: manufacturing, immigration, waterways and transportation, streets and highways, visitors and reception, and last, but not least, advertising. The new Chamber of Commerce building opened its doors at the corner of Brown and Clay Streets with 250 enthusiastic members in attendance.

Each member made a commitment to the 20th century. One participant phrased his millennium prophecy as follows: "The future of Napa County is destined to be a grand one. Her varied resources will always bring into her coffers almost untold wealth. Her wine industry is yet in its infancy. Her agricultural products are almost boundless, and her fine pleasure resorts and grand climate will always attract a host of tourists into her boundaries."

Lee Hart is an expert on George Yount, one of Napa's most famous settlers. Hart dresses authentically down to the last detail and brings history alive by speaking at area schools and historical societies.

A landmark in Napa, the Grape Crusher statue stands tall near the south entrance to Napa Valley.

Nationalities

In 1880, with just over 4,000 voting citizens in Napa County, the residents' origins were as follows:

2,973 U.S. born (of whom only 163 were California born)

1,030 foreign born, including:

333 Irish	26 Swedish
239 German	25 Mexican
100 English	18 Danish
47 Canadian	18 Norwegian
47 Swiss	11 Italian
36 Scottish	2 Chinese, (born of American parents)
33 French	2 born at sea (consequently, able to claim no native land)

The occupations of these citizens included the following:

Farmers: 1653	Saloon-keepers: 24
Mechanics: 807	Clergymen: 21
Day Laborers: 607	Printers: 19
Clerks: 79	Lawyers: 13
Teachers: 41	Law Students: 5
Doctors: 34	Editors: 6

Intricate carvings adorn antique wine barrels on display at Beringer Winery.

"The future of Napa County is destined to be a grand one. Her varied resources will always bring into her coffers almost untold wealth. Her wine industry is yet in its infancy. Her agricultural products are almost boundless, and her fine pleasure resorts and grand climate will always attract a host of tourists into her boundaries."

Member of the newly established Napa Chamber of Commerce,
January, 1904

Napa's earliest white settler, George Yount, is buried in the historic Pioneer Cemetery in Yountville. The Mexican government ceded a 20-square-mile tract to Yount in 1835, and he established the Valley's first vineyard in 1838.

Toni Porterfield visits the grave of her great-great-great-grandfather.

As winter moves into early spring, Napa Valley vineyards once again wear a mantle of vibrant yellow mustard.

CHAPTER 2

Viticulture & Vintners

While dining at a Calistoga hotel, a guest requested a wine with a long French name. The waiter recommended a bottle of Napa Valley wine. But no, the guest knew what California wine was, and refused any of that "sour stuff." The waiter was out of the French brand, but filled an old bottle, with the French label still on it, with wine from a neighboring cellar. The guest was delighted, ordered two bottles instead of one, then inquired where he could purchase more of the superb French claret. Thunderstruck at learning the wine had been made within five miles of town, the humbled diner accompanied the waiter to the wine cellar and ordered a goodly supply. The year was 1880.

In Paris, a wine merchant conducted a blind tasting of 20 wines, white and red, French and Californian, at the Hotel Inter-Continental before an all-French jury. First place in the claret/Cabernet Sauvignon category went to Stag's Leap Wine Cellars of the Napa Valley for a 1973 cabernet made from three-year-old vines. The year was 1976.

When the Vintners Club duplicated the tasting in 1978, nearly 200 judges again ranked Stag's Leap first. In Paris, the Chateau Montelena 1973 Chardonnay of Napa took first place in the white wine category.

In Santa Rosa, California, four panels of American judges tasting American wines were investigating the "terroir" of the wines. In French, "terroir" is the total effect on wine of climate, solar energy, topographical relief, and the soil's basic geology and hydrology—the soil-water relationship. One judge recalled the occasion thus: "I can tell you, it was a humbling experience. Among the first wines we tasted was a flight of 12 red wines, most of which were Cabernet Sauvignons. We sipped, savored, and spit, finally deciding that Cabernet Sauvignon should never be grown in the terroir that produced these hard, humorless wines that lacked fruit and charm. And what is the location of the terroir that nurtured these cabernets? Napa Valley. I mean, as a panel, we were ready for an extra-large slice of humble pie, not to mention the need for a palate transplant." The year was 1999.

Wine appreciation can be both rewarding and confusing. In descending order, the world's top 10 wine-consuming nations in 1996, gallons per capita, were France, Italy, Portugal, Luxembourg, Argentina, Switzerland, Slovenia, Spain, Austria, and Romania. America placed 30th, consuming less than 2 gallons of wine per capita annually, compared with 54 gallons of soft drinks. In 1881, a Napa writer observed, "The majority of Americans are not connoisseurs in wine, and do not know one wine from another. Most Americans like sweet wines, hence the 'dry' wines which should be used at table have never been favorable with them, hence there has been but little demand for wines at the table." Eleven percent of Americans drink 88 percent of American wine. Ninety percent of American wines are made in California, creating an $11 billion wine industry. In 1998, the readers of the *Wine Spectator* voted California as the Best World Region for value wines, and the Napa Valley as Most Favorite Wine Region for vacationing in the world.

By 1997, no other Western Hemisphere appellation, i.e., the specific territory, had a better reputation for wines than the Napa Valley. Warren Winiarski, founder and proprietor of Stag's Leap Wine Cellars, expressed his philosophy in a memorial tribute to another wine visionary, Jack Davies, proprietor of Schramsberg Vineyards:

"Making wine from grapes is, itself, an act of preservation. The art takes the life and sunshine, soul and water of one cycle of the sun, and preserves them in a more sublime form—sometimes for more than man's allotted lifetime. The grape itself, or rather the seed within it, is an expression of the vine's longing for eternity."

Since no two wineries are alike, every winery visit offers a unique experience. Domaine Carneros is a French chateau inspired by the 18th-century Chateau de la Marquetterie, owned by the Taittinger family in Champagne. Also creating sparkling wine, at its location less than a mile away, is Artesa, an underground Catalan castle. When the winery was built, part of a hill was removed and set aside. The visitors center, offices, and the production area were then built on the scooped-out hillside. The reserved earth covered the building as a berm, matching the winery's height with the top of the original hill.

Elaborate wine caves provide another adventure. Schramsberg's were designed in 1870, using Chinese laborers laid off from the transcontinental railway. Stan Anderson's winery contains 10,000 square feet of caves with cathedral-type ceilings measuring up to 22 feet in height. At Shafer Vineyards, fresh underground springs keep cave humidity at 90 percent to prevent wine evaporation. Clos Pegase is a major temple to Bacchus—a cave theater amidst 20,000 square feet of caves. Beringer, Rutherford Hill, Steltzner, Pine Ridge, and Far Niente also maximize underground facilities.

Jarvis Winery resembles a special-effects set from a James Bond film, with 45,000 square feet of floor space carved into the side of a mountain. This cavern contains the entire winemaking processes so that wines never see the light of day until they are shipped. In addition, there is a grand reception hall, the Crystal Chamber, which replicates a portion of the Versailles Hall of Mirrors.

Workers cut back old growth to prepare the grapevines for next year's season.

There are 34,000 acres of grapes and 240

wineries within the 35-mile-long Napa Valley.

Foremost in the Oakville sub-appellation is the Robert Mondavi Winery, the mecca of Napa. Touring and tasting began here in 1966, setting a high standard for the rest of the Valley's wineries to match. Just north in Rutherford is Beaulieu "Beautiful Place" Vineyard, founded in 1900. Across the road is the Niebaum-Coppola Estate Winery, home to filmmaker Francis Ford Coppola. It dates back to 1879 and was started by a Finnish sea captain who founded Inglenook, one of Napa's earliest and most famous wine estates. Next door is Grgich Hills Cellar, named after the winemaker who made the 1973 Chardonnay that won the Judgment of Paris in 1976.

In 1883, two young German immigrants constructed an exact copy of a 17-room castle on the Rhine that they had admired from childhood. This same Rhine House of St. Helena is a must-visit. Within the last decade, two Beringer wines have been named Wine of the Year by *Wine Spectator* magazine: the 1986 Beringer Private Reserve Cabernet Sauvignon and the 1994 Beringer Private Reserve Chardonnay. In 1998, *Wine Spectator* named the 1996 Beringer Private Reserve the number-two white wine in the world and ranked the 1994 Beringer Private Reserve Cabernet Sauvignon in the top 10 of red wines worldwide.

Sterling Vineyards of Calistoga resembles a Greek hilltop monastery, complete with aerial tram leading to the Visitors Center and a spectacular view of the Valley floor. Northward is Chateau Montelena, founded in 1882, a stone winery castle built into the hillside facing Jade Lake. Domaine Carneros and Chateau Montelena can be compared to the South and North bookends that hold all the encyclopedic wine volumes of the Napa Valley. Pleasant reading indeed.

Tanks of wine tower over John Williams, owner/winemaker at Frog's Leap Winery.

According to Robert Parker, known as the most powerful man in the world of wine, "Probably 80 percent of anyone's appreciation of wine is really olfactory or smell, even though we perceive it as taste. Every wine I've ever given 100 points to, I could sense it was worth that the second I smelled it." Two Napa Valley vintners receive superlative praise: Bill Harlan and Helen Turley. Harlan Estate Cabernet is "maybe the single most profound wine in California." Parker has given recent vintages scores of 98, 99, and 100. Turley is his favorite American winemaker. She and her husband, John Wetlaufer, the vineyard manager, make Chardonnays under their own Marcassin label, and are also consultants for Colgin Cellars, Bryant Family Vineyard, Pahlmeyer and Martinelli, and other high-scoring wineries. To Parker, she is a "genius" and a "wine goddess" who makes sensational wines.

As part of the wine-making process, grapes go through a crusher/stemmer.

The Wine and the Wherefore

The Napa Valley Wine Auction, the nation's largest charity wine event, is sponsored annually in the first week of June by the Napa Valley Vintners Association. This professional, nonprofit trade organization represents 156 Napa Valley wineries in marketing and promotional activities throughout the United States and abroad.

The origins of the NVVA go back to 1943, when the Napa Valley wine industry was struggling with problems caused by Prohibition, the Great Depression, and World War II. Four vintners, Louis M. Martini, Louis Stralla, Charles Forni, and John Daniel Jr., decided to establish an association that would foster a consolidation of strength for their local industry.

Wine barrels line the walls of underground tunnels at Beringer Vineyards in St. Helena. The tunnels, made of volcanic ash, were dug by Chinese workers in the 19th century.

By 1971, the Napa County wine grape crop surpassed in value the once-reigning agribusiness of cattle. In 1976, the famous Paris Tasting propelled Napa wines into the global limelight, and in 1978, Napa Valley was officially recognized as an appellation.

In 1980, while discussing the lack of resources for local medical facilities, the idea for the Napa Valley Wine Auction was conceived by Robert Mondavi and Pat Montandon. The first auction was held in 1981. It was attended by 260 bidders who paid $100 for their paddles and spent over $300,000 for the auctioned wines. In 1999, there were 700 paddles at a cost of $1,800 per couple, raising a record-breaking $5.5 million for local charities. Certainly having Robin Williams and Michael Jordan as surprise participants escalated the bidding.

Napa Valley winemaking, coupled with American ingenuity and enterprise, has achieved great results to parallel those of the Wine Auction. Two examples must suffice:

• The Chairman of the 19th Annual Napa Valley Wine Auction, John Shafer of Shafer Vineyards, flew in a World War II squadron led by Jimmy Stewart. It was the lure of Wine Country farming that inspired Shafer in 1972 to make a career change, leaving behind 23 years of publishing experience to begin work in Napa Valley. A different entry level lay beneath his boots as he tilled the soil of his family's new 210-acre estate in the foothills of the Stag's Leap Palisades.

In 1979, much to his wife's consternation, he wrapped barrels of the first "hillside select" Stag's Leap District Cabernet, the '78, in the family's electric blankets to complete malolactic fermentation. In 1993, this same "electric blanket" vintage won an international competition in Germany, outranking such wines as Chateau Margaux and Chateau Latour. Today, the Hillside Select is firmly established as Shafer's signature wine.

• *Wine Spectator* magazine, in its "Top 100 Wines of 1998," gave seventh place in the world to Al Brounstein's Diamond Creek Cabernet Sauvignon Napa Valley Red Rock Terrace 1995. Red Rock Terrace comprises only seven acres of Diamond Creek Vineyards, but its wines age and improve far better than do those of most California labels, irrespective of variety, vintage, or appellation.

V. Sattui Winery, located on White Lane, 1½ miles south of St Helena, is surrounded by vineyards, picnic areas, and scenic landscaping.

At the second Wine Auction, 1982, a case of 1978 Diamond Creek Cabernet Sauvignon was the highest-bid lot. It sold under the gavel for $5,400. At the 19th Wine Auction, 1999, three 1.5 liter bottles of Diamond Creek Vineyards Cabernet Sauvignon from vintages 1992, 1994, 1996, and one 9-liter bottle of 1987 Diamond Creek Vineyards Cabernet Sauvignon, cradled in a hand-forged grapevine motif centerpiece, sold for $130,000. *In vino veritas.*

Wine auction proceeds initially went solely to the Queen of the Valley Hospital and the St. Helena Hospital and Health Center. Today, more than a dozen health-care organizations have been funded, including Clinic Ole, Healthy Moms and Babies, Napa Valley AIDS Project, Napa Valley Community Dental Clinic, Napa Emergency Women's Services, Family Service of the North Bay, and Lutheran Social Services of Northern California. Beginning in 1999, approximately 80 percent of auction proceeds went to health care, either in direct distributions to health-care organizations or to the

Napa Valley Health Care Fund. The remainder was funneled to programs facilitating the creation of low-cost or sustainable farm worker housing and to programs helping children succeed in schools and teens transition into responsible adulthood.

The Health Care Fund is a permanent reserve established in 1989 by the Wine Auction Board of Directors for local health-care programs, in the event of an auction shortfall or community medical emergency. The fund now stands at over $8 million.

With 19 auctions under its belt, the NVVA has raised over $20 million for charitable causes. The NVVA maintains a Web site at www.napavintners.com and a year-round, 24-hour informational hotline at (707) 942-9783, ext. 903.

Chateau Montelena, more than a century old, is on Tubbs Lane in Calistoga. Its wine took first place in the famous Paris Tasting competition of 1976.

John Shafer, chief executive officer of Shafer Vineyards, oversees his vineyards in the Stag's Leap District on the Silverado Trail.

The magnificent gardens at Sutter Home Winery provide a rainbow of color during the summer months.

Selected Tastings and Tours in the Napa Valley

Artesa
Henry Road
Napa

Beaulieu Vineyard
St. Helena Highway
Rutherford

Beringer Wine Estates
Main Street
St. Helena

Carneros Alambic Distillery
Cuttings Wharf Road
Napa

Charles Krug Winery
Main Street
St. Helena

Chateau Montelena
Tubbs Lane
Calistoga

Clos Pegase
Dunaweal Lane
Calistoga

Clos Du Val
Silverado Trail
Napa

Domaine Carneros
Duhig Road
Napa

El Molino Winery
Lyman Canyon Road
St. Helena

Franciscan Estates
Galleron Road
St. Helena

Grgich Hills Cellar
St. Helena Highway
Rutherford

Hakusan Sake Gardens
One Executive Way
Napa

The Hess Collection Winery
Redwood Road
Napa

Jarvis Winery
Monticello Road
Napa

Louis Martini Winery
South St. Helena Highway
St. Helena

Monticello Cellars
Big Ranch Road
Napa

Mumm Napa Valley
Silverado Trail
Rutherford

Newlan Vineyards & Winery
Solano Avenue
Napa

Niebaum-Coppola Estate Winery
St. Helena Highway
Rutherford

Opus One
St. Helena Highway
Oakville

Prager Winery & Port Works
Lewelling Lane
St. Helena

Raymond Vineyard & Cellar
Zinfandel Lane
St. Helena

Robert Mondavi Winery
St. Helena Highway
Oakville

Schramsberg
Schramsberg Road
Calistoga

Shafer Vineyards
Silverado Trail
Napa

Silverado Vineyards
Silverado Trail
Napa

St. Supery Vineyards
St. Helena Highway
Rutherford

V. Sattui Winery
White Lane
St. Helena

Sterling Vineyards
Dunaweal Lane
Calistoga

Sullivan Vineyards
Galleron Lane
Rutherford

Sutter Home Winery
Main Street
St. Helena

Swanson Vineyards
Manley Lane
Rutherford

Trefethen Vineyards
Oak Knoll Avenue
Napa

Trinchero Family Estates
Main Street
St. Helena

Van Der Heyden Vineyards & Winery
Silverado Trail
Napa

William Hill Winery
Atlas Peak Road
Napa

ZD Wines
Silverado Trail
Napa

Marilyn and Ren Harris, owners of Paradigm Vineyards, take a stroll and survey the fruits of their labor.

The Niebaum-Coppola Estate Winery is owned by filmmaker Francis Ford Coppola. It is located in Rutherford and dates back to 1879.

"Making wine from grapes is, itself, an act of preservation. The art

takes the life and sunshine, soul and water of one cycle of the sun, and

preserves them in a more sublime form—sometimes for more than

man's allotted lifetime. "

Warren Winiarski,
founder and proprietor of Stag's Leap Wine Cellars

Sightseers in the Valley can soar in the clouds or take a mountain cable car to Sterling Vineyards.

The Valley's Regions of Viniculture

Carneros

Topography: Vineyards in this southernmost appellation encompass parts of Napa and Sonoma counties. The gently rolling land disappears into San Pablo Bay. The moderating influence of the maritime climate is key to the distinct character of wines made from Carneros grapes.
Varieties: Chardonnay (nearly half of the appellation yield), Gewurztraminer, Riesling, Cabernet Sauvignon, Merlot, and Pinot Noir. The blend of Carneros Chardonnays and Pinots is an excellent base for sparkling wines.
Distinction: Rich Burgundian Chardonnays; crisp, fresh Gewurztraminer and Riesling; spicy reds.

Mount Veeder

Topography: With its southern location and numerous microclimates, the Mount Veeder appellation combines elevation, location, and excellent exposure to give ideal cool-growing conditions, which produce a complexity and concentration of fruit. The soil is a combination of sandstone and light clay, which yields cassis or black fruit flavors.
Varieties: Cabernet and Chardonnay.
Distinction: Briary, woody, possibly due to the forested region. Deep colors.

Wild Horse Valley

Topography: High, narrow saddle of land above the Valley floor with shallow, well-drained soils containing a mixture of volcanic and sedimentary soil high in minerals.
Varieties: Chardonnay and Pinot Noir.
Distinction: Long ripening season produces bright, fruity flavors.

Atlas Peak District

Topography: Volcanic, rocky soil and acceptable drainage. The climate here is cooler than northern Napa Valley appellations. The cool night air on the Valley floor causes heat inversion on the hillsides, yielding a broad temperature profile.
Varieties: Sangiovese, Cabernet Sauvignon, and Chardonnay (and, in trial amounts: Sauvignon Blanc, Semillon, Pinot Blanc).
Distinction: Full-bodied reds of distinction.

Stag's Leap District

Topography: An alluvial stretch of land descending from the foot of the eastern Palisades to the east bank of the Napa River.
Varieties: Cabernet Sauvignon and other Bordeaux-type grapes.
Distinction: The tannin structure is the dominant attribute that sets Stag's Leap wines apart. Drinkable early on, but will age.

Oakville

Topography: Shaped like a shallow bowl with gravelly and alluvial shallow loams on the western benchlands and alternating bands of silt, sand, and gravel in deeper soils along the Napa River.

Varieties: Cabernet Sauvignon and Chardonnay, some Merlot and Cabernet Franc.

Distinction: Spicy, fruity, well-balanced red wines and luscious, fruity whites.

Rutherford

Topography: A continuation of the Oakville topography, with a large alluvial fan on the western benchland; silt, sand, and gravel along the Napa River; and clay soils on the eastern portion.

Varieties: Cabernet Sauvignon and Chardonnay, much like Oakville.

Distinction: Concentrated fruit with a mineral-like "dusty" quality in the reds. The whites are similar to Oakville's, but more austere.

Howell Mountain

Topography: Elevated plateau, with some hilly portions. The soils on Howell Mountain are mostly volcanic in origin.

Varieties: Cabernet Sauvignon, Zinfandel, and Chardonnay, with minor plantings of other reds and whites.

Distinction: Rich Chardonnays, with an interesting mineral quality; big, robust Cabernets; and juicy Zinfandels.

Spring Mountain District

Topography: Mountainous with poor, eroded soils of widely differing types.

Varieties: Primarily Cabernet Sauvignon, Merlot, and Cabernet Franc, with lesser amounts of other reds and whites.

Distinction: Full-bodied and tannic; flavorful, but not overly fruity wines.

CHAPTER 3

A Cluster
of Choices

Balloon tours offer a dramatic vantage point to view the valley's vineyards.

The Napa Valley land-ladder features 30 miles of historic sites and regional attractions.

© Bear Productions, 1999

Imagine the Napa Valley as a north-south, 30-mile-long land-ladder of opportunities and attractions—a ladder braced strongly by 20 horizontal east-west county and city road rungs. The ladder's left leg is Highway 29; the right is the Silverado Trail. The top rung is Tubbs Lane, Calistoga; the bottom rung is Highway 12, also known as the Carneros Highway. One carefree way to enjoy the land-ladder is to ride the Napa Valley Wine Train from Napa to St. Helena and back with a stop in Yountville. Whether for lunch or dinner, this is a three-hour excursion aboard lavishly restored vintage, turn-of-the-century Pullman cars replete with swivel lounge chairs, loveseats, rich polished woods, and etched-glass windows. An alternate way is to start by car at the top of the land-ladder and proceed side-to-side and downward.

The Old Faithful Geyser in California, one of only three Old Faithful Geysers in the world, is located conveniently at 1299 Tubbs Lane. Its steaming waterspout erupts approximately every 40 minutes, 60 feet high, spraying 4,000 sulphurous gallons each time. Thanks to a clock announcing the next eruption, you have time to visit the world-famous winery Chateau Montelena next door or the Robert Pecota Winery on Bennett Lane, or Vincent Arroyo Winery on Greenwood Avenue before or after Old Faithful's showtime.

Six miles west of Old Faithful are the world's largest petrified trees. Over three million years ago, a volcanic blast in the direction of Mt. St. Helena erupted seven miles northeast of here. The blast covered the slopes of the mountain with a thick layer of lava and ash. Heavy rains turned the mountainside into a massive river of mud. The force of the blast flattened and buried the forest in a deep layer of mineral-rich, muddy ash. This same pale yellow, sandy ash is the soil you walk on today at the Petrified Forest. All the petrified treetops point in a southwest direction away from the volcano, supporting the theory that the blast knocked the trees over. Most of these redwoods were already more than 2,000 years old when they were buried. One of them, the "Monarch," was 300 feet high. A third of the Monarch has been exposed to date, six feet in diameter, complete with petrified bark.

At the intersection of Highway 29 and the Silverado Trail is the trailhead to the Oat Hill Mine Road, considered by some as the most spectacular day hike in the whole Napa Valley. Over a century old, it merges with the new Palisades Trail alignment into Robert Louis Stevenson State Park. And, after the hike, you can relax in a Calistoga whirlpool of subterranean hot springs, or indulge in a therapeutic mudbath of volcanic ash and peat moss, and then dine in the neighborhood—a perfect conclusion to a superlative day.

The Sharpsteen Museum, on Washington Street in Calistoga, is the creation of Ben Sharpsteen, Oscar-winning producer and Walt Disney Studios animator. His three-dimensional dioramas transport one back to the elegant 1860s Hot Springs resort of pioneer, promoter, publisher, entrepreneur, and soldier-of-fortune Sam Brannan, who christened Calistoga as the Saratoga of California.

Ten minutes south of the museum, on Highway 29, is Bothe-Napa Valley State Park, an 1,800-acre park offering camping, swimming, hiking, horseback riding, cooking areas, picnic tables, and showers. There are stands of coastal redwoods, Douglas Fir, tan oak, madrone, and a clear lookout from Coyote Peak on the Coyote Peak/Redwood Trail Loop, a five-mile hike lasting about three hours. Elevations range from 400 to 2,000 feet.

Bale Grist Mill State Historic Park lies directly below Bothe-Napa Valley State Park, just three miles north of St. Helena. The mill's 36-foot overshot waterwheel provided the power to grind wheat in the mid-19th century for local communities. Visitors can witness the mill's original quartz stones at work while naturalists will be able to count up to 20 different trees in both parks.

Across the highway is Hurd Beeswax Candles, a popular destination for 40 years. Sheets of parchment beeswax are first softened, then hand-rolled into the desired thickness. This small visitor-friendly workshop demonstrates how

skilled artisans have mastered every phase of candlemaking with hands-on expertise. To quote one worker: "We have more beeswax candles than you can shake a wick at."

The Culinary Institute of America, also known as the other CIA, is situated inside the old Christian Brothers Winery on North Main Street, St. Helena. A more solid edifice cannot be found in all of Napa County. When erected in 1889, it became the world's largest stone winery, three stories high, 80-by-400 feet, with walls three feet thick. Known as Greystone Cellars and under the direction of Brother Timothy, its blended wines could always be relied upon for consistent excellence. Now it is home to a famous culinary academy of equally high standards. In March 1999, an American baking team captured for the first time the grand prize in the 1999 World Cup Baking Competition in Paris. Two members of the three-man team were from the CIA; Robert Jorin and Thomas Gumpel both are chefs and teaching instructors at the institute. This is an additional incentive to sample the year-round experimental menus for global appetites offered by the Greystone Restaurant.

Every 40 minutes, the Old Faithful Geyser of California blasts a 60-foot-high tower of water and steam. The Geyser is located one mile north of Calistoga on Tubbs Lane.

Diamond Creek, owned by Al Brounstein, produces cabernet sauvignon with a worldwide reputation for excellence.

Napa County's Italian heritage can be tasted throughout the valley, from its oldest restaurant, the Depot in Napa, to the Napa Valley Olive Oil Manufactory in St. Helena. While the Depot has been operating continuously for 75 years, the Manufactory has been bottling and selling olive oils for 32 years. Stepping into either establishment is an immediate reentry to Tuscany.

Seasonally fresh produce is monitored by the Napa County Farm Bureau through its publication, *Napa County Farming Trails*. The following harvest calendar testifies to the Valley's bountiful diversity:

- Apples (July-October)
- Basil (June-September)
- Berries (June-July)
- Figs (September-November)
- Grapes (September-October)
- Nectarines (April-September)
- Peaches (July-August)
- Pears (August-October)
- Persimmons (November)
- Plums (July-August)
- Pumpkins (October)
- Tomatoes (August-October)
- Vegetables (June-October)
- Walnuts (October-December)

Calistoga, St. Helena, Yountville, and Napa all have colorful weekly Farmers Markets from May through November. On May 10, 1877, a Scottish visitor to the Napa Valley sent the following letter home: "Napa Valley is a wonderfully nice place. They have all their rain in winter and never any at all in summer. They have always plenty and never too much rain for their crops. This dry air makes the valley suitable for wine grapes grown in great quantities, whole tracts being covered with the vines. It is never very cold in winter and in the middle of summer they need blankets at night. There is a land for you." In the year 2000, not a word of this letter needs changing.

There are, of course, many delightful hotels, B&Bs, and inns stretched up and down the Napa Valley land-ladder. The Napa Valley Conference and Visitors Bureau offers free planning assistance at 1310 Napa Town Center. The Conference Services Department can be reached Monday through Friday from 9 A.M. to 5 P.M. (Pacific Time) at (707) 226-3610. The Bureau can also give restaurant advice and information in general regarding outdoor activities such as fishing, canoeing, ballooning, bicycling, croquet, gliding, hiking, petanque, horseback riding, tennis, and golf. There are, for example, nine golf courses in the Napa Valley: Aetna Springs, Chardonnay Golf Course, Chimney Rock Golf Course, Meadowood Resort Hotel, Mt. St. Helena Golf Course, Napa Municipal Golf Course, Napa Valley Country Club, the Silverado Country Club, and the Yountville Golf Course.

Yountville is home to the French Laundry Restaurant on Washington. You won't spot a sign for it, even though chef-owner Thomas Keller was named American Chef of the Year 1998 by the James Beard Foundation. Dinner reservations usually require two months' advance booking, but lucky cancellations do occur. Nearby, at 55 Presidents Circle, is the Napa Valley Museum, a non-profit cultural institution that recognizes, celebrates, and advances the unique historical, artistic, and environmental heritage of the Napa region. The Museum's primary purpose is to provide enjoyable, interactive educational experiences and to collect, conserve, and exhibit objects relevant to the area. Special areas of interest include geography, geology, Wappo Native Americans, Mexican Rancho Days, pioneers, the Chinese, ranching, farming, viticulture, wine, mining, transportation, and hot springs resorts.

Finally, on the southernmost rung of the Napa Valley land-ladder, is the di Rosa Preserve of Art & Nature, on the Carneros Highway. A museum of art produced in the greater San Francisco Bay Area during the latter part of the 20th century, it depicts more than 1,500 works by over 600 artists in four rustic galleries and a huge sculpture meadow. All of the art has been described by Rene di Rosa as "Divinely Regional, Superbly Parochial, Wondrously Provincial: An Absolute Native Glory." The museum tour, inside and outdoors, takes over two hours for an initial browse-through. With rolling countryside and a 35-acre lake surrounding the galleries, the artistic experiences are breathtaking.

Calistoga's famous mud baths, mixed from volcanic ash and peat moss, are a soothing treat for tired travelers.

Runners participate in the annual Sutter Home Napa Valley Marathon, held in Napa on the first Sunday in March. The competition is limited to 1,800 entrants.

Every March, cyclists gather in Napa to participate in World Cup bicycling events.

Lake Berryessa is a popular spot for fans of all water sports.

The Napa Valley Wine Train
makes three-hour round-trip
excursions from Napa to St.
Helena with a stop in
Yountville. The train features
lavishly restored, antique
Pullman cars.

The bees stay busy at Hurd Beeswax Candles, where skilled artisans have been making handrolled candles for more than 40 years.

A variety of produce can be purchased year-round at the farmers market at Crane Park. In addition to grapes, seasonal offerings include peaches, pears, tomatoes, and pumpkins.

The valley offers a variety of outdoor recreational activities, including horseback riding and hiking.

The Napa Valley is home to nine golf courses, including one at the Silverado Country Club.

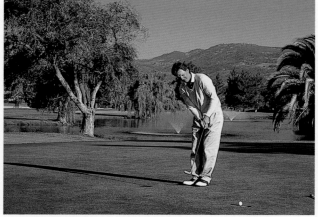

At the intersection of Highway 29 and the Silverado Trail is the trailhead to the Oat Hill Mine Road, considered by some as the most spectacular day hike in the whole Napa Valley. Over a century old, it merges with the new Palisades Trail alignment into Robert Louis Stevenson State Park.

Above: Guests are surrounded by glitz and glamour during a wine-tasting party at ZD Winery.

Right: Robert Jörin, a Swiss chef at the Culinary Institute, earned the prestigious Coupe de Monde de la Boulangerie in 1999. This international award also is known as "The World Cup of Bread."

The Napa Valley Wine Auction at Meadowood, the nation's largest charity wine event, is sponsored annually in the first week of June by the Napa Valley Vintners Association. After 19 auctions, the NVVA has raised over $20 million for charitable causes.

The Culinary Institute of America is located in the Greystone Winery, a century-old structure that once housed the Christian Brothers Winery. One of the world's leading schools for chefs is located at the institute.

Right: Ca Toga Art, a gallery in Calistoga, features the art of owner Carlo Marchiori. Here, visitors will find a wide array of artistic presentations, including painted ceilings, sculpture, ceramics, and paintings.

Below: At the Rene di Rosa Preserve of Art and Nature, works are displayed in a huge sculpture meadow and in four galleries. This extraordinary museum of art can be found on the Carneros Highway. The sculpture titled "Endless Summer" was created by Rene di Rosa's late wife, Veronica di Rosa.

A wide variety of sculptures are on view at the Rene di Rosa Preserve of Art, including "Figure of Speech" by Robert Hudson.

"Reclining Nude #2" by Viola Frey is among more than 1,500 works by hundreds of artists on display at the di Rosa Preserve of Art.

CHAPTER 4

Grape Expectations

"Standing on the Corner, Watching All the Girls Go By" is a song title from the 1956 Frank Loesser musical *The Most Happy Fella*. To be specific, the corner is located at the intersection of First Street and Main Street in downtown Napa. An Italian-American grape grower named Tony is the happiest guy in the whole Napa Valley as he awaits the arrival of Rosabella, his intended bride.

On the south side of First Street, two doors east of Main, stands the Semorile Building, a delicate Italianate composition designed by architect Luther Turton and constructed by William Bradford at a cost of $6,700 for the Italian-American greengrocer Bartolomeo Semorile, his wife, Emily, and their family. The grocery store occupied the first story; living quarters were on the second. Cast iron Corinthian columns at the first floor, the iron balcony railing, and the iron balustrade crowning the parapet produce an almost fragile appearance. The second floor is symmetrical above the central door. Arched openings that once held stained glass transom windows and carved keystones accent the center of each arch. Many Napa residents consider the Semorile Building to be one of the most beautiful in downtown Napa. Just around the corner on Main is another Italianate two-story structure, the Winship Building, also built in 1888. Once the tallest building on Main Street, its tower was removed in 1910.

Continuing in a westward direction, a walking tour brings you to the First National Bank Building on First Street, home to Napa County Landmarks, a community resource center, and one of the few neoclassical structures in the county. The terra cotta brick exterior is accented by Corinthian columns and an elaborate cornice exhibiting dentil work and egg-and-dart molding. Just down the street is the Gordon Building, built in 1929 with Art Deco influences such as a colorful facade of glazed terra cotta tiles. The Hayes and

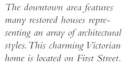

The downtown area features many restored houses representing an array of architectural styles. This charming Victorian home is located on First Street.

Empire theaters once occupied the site, offering vaudeville and early cinema. Samuel Gordon, a Russian immigrant and early commercial developer erected the present structure for Bryant's Candy Store.

Continuing in this direction, you'll find the Napa Register Building, built in 1905 by George Francis to house the *Napa Register* downstairs, with offices and a dance studio above. Across the road is the beloved Goodman Library, built in 1901 out of native stone for $15,000. This library was a gift to the community from pioneer banker George E. Goodman, who co-owned Napa's first bank, the Goodman Bank. Also designed by Luther Turton, the library opened as the Goodman Library, Tea, and Rest Room. The classical use of native stone in the columns and balustrade gives the building a rough, heavy feeling of the Romanesque style popularized in the 1880s by the eastern architect Henry Hobson Richardson.

The Goodman serves as headquarters for the Napa County Historical Society, first organized in May 1948 at a pioneer picnic at the Old Bale Mill and incorporated six days later. The Society was established to study the history of California and especially of the Napa Valley. Its projects include the collection, preservation, organization, and sharing of information and artifacts of historical value, and its mission is to bring the rich heritage of this fascinating region to public awareness.

The research library has books on California and Napa Valley history, old city directories, many original manuscripts, hundreds of old photographs of pioneer settlers and historical sites, and thousands of newspaper clippings pertaining to local history and residents. There are also old maps, architectural plans, and videos. Library users also may hear first-hand accounts from older members of the Society, who are sharing their memories with researchers and the younger generations. These reminiscences are currently being collected and preserved on audiotapes by the Society's Oral History Committee.

The museum houses such varied artifacts as historical documents, period clothing (especially Chinese clothing), old pistols, stationeries of old Napa Valley businesses, political buttons, authentic Indian baskets, old grocery baskets, and pressed native plants. The Society's offices, research library, and museum are open to the public without charge every Tuesday and Thursday (except holidays) from noon to 4 P.M.

By the 1870s, the offspring of early Napa business and civic leaders began looking west of Jefferson Street for suitable building sites. In the area along First Street once referred to as "West Napa," they constructed many outstanding examples of Queen Anne, Colonial Revival, Eastlake, and Spanish Colonial Revival styles of architecture.

At 1750 First stands the Noyes Mansion, a 1902 example of Colonial Revival architecture. The rectangular plan, hipped roof, and symmetrical facades with projecting central portion are characteristic of this style. The home was designed by Luther Turton for Frank Noyes, founder of the Noyes Lumber Yard. Across the road is a shingle-style home built between 1915 and 1920. This home departs from the typical shingle style in that the porch is covered by a roof that is separated from the main roof of the house. Influences of stick style are evident in the structural expression of the beam-column connection at the front porch.

The Goodman Library was built in 1901 at a cost of $15,000. Designed by architect Luther Turton, the building features the classical use of native stone.

The Napa Valley Opera House, which presented family entertainment during the frontier days, has been closed since 1914. After an extensive renovation, it will reopen as the Margrit Biever Mondavi Theatre.

The Blue Violet Mansion on Brown Street, once a rundown apartment building, has been restored to its original splendor.

The Noyes House on Jefferson Street at the corner of First, is an 1892 version of Queen Anne style. Virtually unaltered, the house displays the major Queen Anne influences of varied exterior surfaces of shiplap, fishscale, and octagon shingle siding; a steep multiple gable roof with prominent triangular pediments; and an ornamental brick chimney. The large palm trees surrounding the house were planted in 1895. The bungalow-style house at 1834 First, known as the Welti House, was built in 1915. It demonstrates how effectively the characteristics of a bungalow can be assimilated into a larger, two-story home. The brackets supporting the eaves, the battered porch piers, and extended portico over the driveway are typical, as is the garage to the rear.

Across the road at 1801 First is a shingle-style house designed by William Corlett in 1905. Known as the Prouty House, it shows a strong Queen Anne influence in the multigabled roof with its wood cresting and rounded bay window tipped with a conical roof. The strong horizontal lines defined in the dentiled cornice, window detailing, and shingled wall surface classify it as shingle style. In contrast is the Dempsey House at 1827-1831 First. The home, built between 1895 and 1905, is an excellent example of the transition from Queen Anne to the simpler shingle style. A minimal amount of Victorian ornamentation is seen in the pediment over the porch. The corner turret is a design element employed in the later phase of the Queen Anne style as well as in the many buildings in the shingle style.

The Beazley House, 1905, an example of shingle/colonial revival, stands at 1910 First. Designed by Turton, the shingle style is illustrated in the uniform covering of shingles and simple eave treatment. The colonial revival influence reflects the Georgian period with its hip roof, rectangular shape, and symmetrical design. Note variations in the bay window treatments, the stained glass half-round windows, and entrance portico. The original barn-carriage house remains at the rear of the property, and the stone carriage step is on Warren Street. Adjacent is the Francis House at 1926 First, also designed in 1905 by Turton. This structure demonstrates design variations within the framework of the shingle style. Twin dormers in the steeply pitched roof and the shingled gable end facing the street are characteristic, as is the narrow horizontal wood siding and recessed porch.

Across the street is the Smith House, 1875, at 1929 First. This fine example of the Second Empire style carries the hallmark of the high concave mansard roof with dormer windows. The main cornice of the house is distinguished by the paneled frieze and large pierced brackets. Also characteristic are the slanted bay windows flanking the portico over the recessed and paneled entryway. The owners are Doris and Elbert Dawson. Wanting guests to enter the home as if they are entering another century, she restored all 72 windows to their original format. Restoration work has taken more than a decade at a price well over $200,000. "I don't know what to call it," she jokes, "maybe insanity".

Also built in 1875 is the Trubody House at 2021 First. The characteristic square tower of the Italian villa style is only hinted at in the slightly projecting central facade with its triangular pediment. Distinctive features are the cornice with its brackets and paneled frieze and squeezed pedimented window hood on the segmented arched windows, and the one-story bay window with upper sashes of stained glass.

Within the city limits, there are 31 properties listed on the National Register of Historic Places. The Napa County Historic Resources Survey incorporated 154 historic and architecturally significant sites in the county that were identified in 1974-75 by the Historic Preservation and Heritage Committee.

Upon a return to First and Main, one gains an additional appreciation for restoration, renovation, and revitalization when viewing the Margrit Biever Mondavi Theatre at the Opera House at 1018 Main, near the Semorile Building on First Street. As if

The Blue Violet Mansion now serves as a bed-and-breakfast. Its owners spent a decade renovating the home and surrounding garden.

Grounds of the American Center will offer visitors many opportunities to relax and reflect. Illustrations courtesy of The American Center for Wine, Food and the Arts

"This unique educational center will be a place where American music is played, artists-in-residence work, vineyards grow, wonderful meals are created, and visitors and scholars alike explore the richness of America's cultural heritage. A very special place to explore and celebrate the American passion for living well."

Robert Mondavi,
owner, Robert Mondavi Winery

Officials participate in the groundbreaking ceremony for the American Center for Wine, Food and the Arts. Construction on the two-story building and surrounding gardens is estimated at $70 million.

history is repeating itself, the Theatre will be named after the wife of yet another prominent Italian-American, a most happy fella indeed! Final reconstruction is expected to permit the reopening of the theater in 2002. It has been closed since 1914. It was designed in 1879 in the Italianate style by Samuel and Joseph Newsome and flourished as a venue for vaudeville acts, political rallies, local dance recitals, gala masked balls, tours of John Philip Sousa's band, and readings by Jack London. The Opera House never presented opera. Rather, its name was derived during the frontier days as a respectable establishment that ladies and families could patronize. The theater is truly a "grape expectation" for the millennium; without the generosity of wine "angels" such as Robert Mondavi and Joseph Phelps and other community leaders, the $8 million price tag to bring the theater up to code and standards for the millennium would have been impossibly daunting. Perhaps *The Most Happy Fella* will grace the stage in the not-too-distant future.

The rear of the theater overlooks China Point Park. Begun in 1851 as an encampment along the Napa River east of Napa Creek, Chinatown was home to several generations of Chinese immigrants who built early wine caves and worked in pioneer industries. The community once numbered more than 500 residents. Its demise occurred in 1929, when the city bought the land for a yacht harbor that never materialized.

Seventy years later, "The riverfront is going to be a new front door to Napa," says design consultant Terry Bottomley. Construction of a new First Street bridge, estimated to cost $4,000,000, is planned for 2003. The City's General Plan, Envision Napa 2020, contains broad policies to make downtown and the riverfront area a showpiece for the city and the Napa Valley. While the Flood Control Project moves upriver with its five- to seven-year construction schedule, the city will be focusing its efforts on a Downtown Reinvestment Strategy.

The largest linchpin in this Strategy is the forthcoming American Center for Wine, Food and the Arts, a $70 million project spearheaded by Robert Mondavi. The Center is a 75,000-square-foot, two-story education complex surrounded by gardens and scheduled to open Thanksgiving 2001. First Street between China Point Park and the Center is to be upgraded with new sidewalks, landscaping, Victorian-style streetlights and benches, and entry icons for downtown Napa. Luther Turton would be smiling with pleasure and anticipation.

The beautification of First Street will help recreate strength down center of Napa City's most important street rung on the Napa Valley landladder—a one-and-a-half mile rung between the Napa Premium Outlets, all 50 stores, at Highway 29, and the American Center at the Silverado Trail. A complete makeover of First Street between downtown and McKinstry awaits completion of the Napa River Flood Control Project in 2004. Moving all city utility lines underground is a top priority.

Slow but sure growth has been a constant ideal paradigm for Napa City as well as the Valley's vineyards. The American Center will be the Napa Valley in a microcosm. In the words of Robert Mondavi: "This unique educational center will be a place where American music is played, artists-in-residence work, vineyards grow, wonderful meals are created, and visitors and scholars alike explore the richness of America's cultural heritage. A very special place to explore and celebrate the American passion for living well." From the Semorile Building to the American Center, Napa Valley's things of beauty are, indeed, joys forever.

The Napa National Bank
was built in 1923 as the
Bank of Napa. Inspired by
the École des Beaux Arts in
Paris, this Classical Revival
building has six colossal
Doric columns framing the
windows at 903 Main Street.

The Hatt Building, located
in downtown Napa, will
house shops when renovation
is completed.

*China Point Park has a
prominent role in the revitalization of Napa's riverfront.
The area, once known as
Chinatown, was home to
several generations of
Chinese immigrants.*

Epilogue

We hope you have enjoyed this portion of your picturesque tour of Napa. Believe me when I tell you that there is much more to see, and all of it just as beautiful as what you've seen so far. As you continue your *Picture Perfect* tour, you will have the opportunity to see some of the business community and how this element of Napa has served to enrich the lives of our residents. The diversity of Napa is part of the intrigue of our town—the mixture of history and high tech, agriculture and artistry, professionalism and small-town caring. All these things combine to make Napa a truly wondrous place to visit or live.

Of course, the one thing you can't really get a feel for while looking at this lovely book is the uniqueness of the people who reside in Napa. Only in person can you experience the warmth and charm that the inhabitants of Napa offer. In Napa, great things are accomplished through cooperation and a sense of community spirit. Their dedication to the preservation of Napa's history and character as well as to the economic health of the town is just one of the reasons Napa is a unique American city.

Thank you for taking a moment to glimpse the wonders of Napa. We've enjoyed having you visit, and we extend a warm welcome to you for the next time—whether it is within this book or in person.

Sincerely,
Kate King
Executive Director
Napa Chamber of Commerce

Part Two

CHAPTER 5

The Wine Industry

Sutter Home Winery

The Sutter Home story begins in 1874, when groves of prune, walnut, and apple trees were Napa Valley's agricultural livelihood, and only a few vintners were beginning to explore the area's potential as a fine wine-producing region. John Thomann, a Swiss immigrant, built the original winery facility and quickly turned the John Thomann Winery and Distillery into one of the biggest producers of wine in the Valley. Though the winery prospered well into the last part of the century, it was abandoned by the family after John died suddenly of a heart attack while in Switzerland in 1900. The winery remained unused until another Swiss family, the Leuenbergers, who owned and operated a winery on Deer Park Road in St. Helena, bought the Thomann winery facility at a sheriff's sale in 1906 for ten dollars in gold. Their winery was called Sutter Home, after Caroline Leuenberger's father. Caroline, a prominent San Francisco dressmaker, and her husband, Emil, ran the winery until the start of Prohibition. However, by the time the ban on alcohol ended in 1933 they were quite elderly and opted not to reopen the winery. The Sutter Home facility seemed doomed to be continuously rescued and then abandoned.

In 1945, Sutter Home found the good family it needed: the Trincheros, originally from the Asti region of Italy, had migrated to the United States in the 1920s, settling in New York and New Jersey.

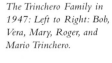

The Trinchero Family in 1947: Left to Right: Bob, Vera, Mary, Roger, and Mario Trinchero.

The family worked as restaurateurs and bartenders, even running an inn and speakeasy in upstate New York during Prohibition. John Trinchero was a winemaker in New Jersey, buying bulk wine from California which was shipped to New Jersey and bottled there. On a business trip to California in 1945, John was driving through the Napa Valley, saw the abandoned winery, and promptly fell in love. He decided to pull up stakes and move to California.

Initially John began by running the winery with a partner; however, the partner bailed out of the project after a few months, and finding himself in need of help, John called his brother Mario back in Manhattan. Mario was hesitant about his brother's plan: he had a wife, three children, and a comfortable city life. However, John was insistent and Mario came out in the summer of 1948 to help his brother with the first crush. That December the rest of Mario's family followed, including his sons, Bob (Sutter Home's current CEO) and Roger; his daughter, Vera; and his wife, Mary. The family began a new life as vintners in a small-town setting that was a world away from Manhattan.

During the late '40s to the early '80s, the Trincheros' winery was the quintessential small, hand-to-mouth family operation: everybody in the family worked in the winery, including the children, who worked after school and on the weekends. For thirty-five years, their method of production did not change. They made a variety of inexpensive, generic wines; however, when John Trinchero retired as winemaker in 1960 and his nephew Bob took the post, Sutter Home was due for a change. To upgrade the quality of Sutter Home wine, Bob began eliminating the jug wines and replacing them with pure varietal wines. He had also discovered zinfandel grapes grown from old vines up in the Sierra foothills, which produced a wine that was dark, fruity, and full-bodied. In 1968, Bob made the winery's first zinfandel from twenty tons of zinfandel grapes he had purchased from Amador County.

Named in honor of Mario Trinchero, M. Trinchero is a reflection of Sutter Home's commitment to produce superior wines.

The Sutter Home Victorian Inn, used for hospitality events, was the enchanting original family home of John Thomann.

The results were magnificent. Bob produced a wine that was big-bodied and intense, one of the best zinfandels that anyone had tasted. The equal of many cabernets then on the market, Sutter Home's zinfandel put Amador County on the wine map and convinced many people that zinfandel grapes, which were then considered good only for blending with others to produce a hearty, generic wine, could indeed produce a first-class varietal wine. Its success also gave Bob the confidence in his own ability to experiment further. Wanting to concentrate on making zinfandel, he struck an agreement with his father, who shared responsibility for the winery, that as zinfandel sales grew, he could delete other wines from their portfolio. Though Mario resisted at first, Bob's conviction proved correct and the winery continued to prosper from zinfandel sales.

Inspired by Sutter Home's success, other wineries began making similar big-bodied, intense zinfandels. By 1972, a handful of wine producers were attempting to out-zinfandel each other by producing the biggest, darkest, most alcoholic zinfandel they could. Bob's technique for creating a more intense zinfandel was to draw off some of the free-run juice at the crusher prior to fermentation; since most of the color and body comes from the skins, increasing the skin-to-juice ratio produces a more intense wine. However, this technique left him with about five hundred gallons of apparently useless pale pink juice; not knowing what to do with it, he fermented it to dryness, put it in barrels, and began selling it in the tasting room as a novelty item. Bob originally called it Oeil de Pedrix: "Eye of the Partridge," the French term for wines with a slight blush of color; however, the BATF insisted on a name that provided a description of its contents for label approval, so Bob appended the name "white zinfandel."

For the first two years, Sutter Home White Zinfandel was not very popular: most people thought it was too dry, and sales were insignificant. However, in 1975, Bob had a stuck fermentation, meaning not all the sugar from the grapes would convert to alcohol. He bottled it up anyway, and though the difference between that batch and past batches was minute (about two percent residual sugar more than usual), the eventual result was phenomenal. The extra sugar took off the dry edge that many found disagreeable, and sales began growing exponentially. White zinfandel was the right wine at the right time. Its fruity taste and freshness appealed to many American consumers whose palates were not accustomed to dry, heavy wines. By 1980, Sutter Home was making about 25,000 cases a year; by 1985, 1.5 million cases; by 1990, 3 million. The runoff from the Trincheros' first phenomenal success had turned into their second, transforming a small family winery into an enormously prosperous, nationwide business in the brief space of ten years. During the 1980s the family purchased acreage throughout the state and began planting different varietals so their offerings would include a full range of

The current generation of Trincheros; Bob Trinchero (Sutter Home's CEO), with sister Vera Trinchero Torres (winery secretary), and brother Roger Trinchero (winery president).

The Sutter Home Garden allows tourists to relax while sampling a variety of famous wines.

varietal wines. They also acquired new facilities to handle increasing production, warehousing, and shipping needs.

As the fourth largest winery and the single top-selling brand of wine in the country, Sutter Home has become known as a company that is willing to step outside the boundaries of tradition. The success of its white zinfandel went completely against the upper-echelon ideal of a wine that is oak-aged, dry, and rich. By eschewing convention and peeling away the mystery that surrounds wine service, Sutter Home has enabled more consumers to enjoy drinking wine; by paying attention to how people drink wine, the winery has attracted a broader consumer base that keeps it in the vanguard of wine sales.

The past two decades have seen many examples of Sutter Home's willingness to take risks, creating products and packaging designed to get people more interested and more comfortable with the wine-drinking experience. During the 1980s more people were living alone and drinking moderately, a combination which hindered many from buying a whole bottle for fear of it going to waste. Seeing this, Sutter Home began marketing their premium wines in small bottles, perfect for a single serving; the 'Classic

Singles' which came out in 1989 were the perfect answer to the 1980s' mood of moderation. It was also the first time Sutter Home introduced their Vin-Loc™ bottle closure. Wine is the only mass-marketed beverage that requires an opener, and research showed that very few households keep a corkscrew. For this reason, when Sutter Home introduced the liter-and-a-half magnum size for the first time in 1993, they decided to seal it with a Vin-Loc™ closure instead of a cork, the first premium wine producer to do so. Screw-top closures have been found to be much more reliable than corks, which can crack, crumble, or pick up moldy smells, thus rendering the wine undrinkable.

In 1991, information about the salubrious health benefits of red wine was beginning to break out from the industry into the main-stream media. This knowledge, and the fact that many of Sutter Home's customers had been drinking white zinfandel for almost 20 years and their tastes were becoming more sophisticated, suggested developing a red wine that would be palatable for customers who enjoyed Sutter Home's other highly accessible wines. Their answer to this scenario was Soléo, a chillable red wine made from a propri-etary blend of zinfandel, barbera, and pinot noir which began a

The Soléo web page features bright graphics, music, and animation.

light red wine category of beaujolais-style wines that became increasingly popular in the early 1990s. And in 1998, Sutter Home introduced three varieties of fruit-flavored zinfandels called Portico, over 99 percent wine with natural fruit flavors. Like white zinfandel, Portico is a product that will introduce non-wine drinkers to wine and provide a bridge for blush wine drinkers to red wine.

Rather than compete with other large premium wineries for a share of a small, static market, Sutter Home is striving to reach the average American consumer. Yet rather than sacrifice quality for accessibility, Sutter Home continues to produce a range of fine varieties. The winery just released a new ultra-premium brand called M. Trinchero, in honor of Mario Trinchero, with a chardonnay and a cabernet sauvignon made exclusively from Napa Valley grapes. It is both a testament to Mario Trinchero's passion for the wine industry and his family's affection toward him, as well as a reflection of Sutter Home's continuing commitment to produce complex, exciting wines.

During the busy summer season, the bar in Sutter Home's St. Helena tasting room and retail store, the original Thomann winery facility, is often crowded three-deep with tasters eager to sample Sutter Home wine. The Trincheros' ability to make a wine for every taste is an admirable feat which they continue to accomplish with grace and resolve. The evolution of Sutter Home from a small family-run winery to the number one selling brand in the country parallels the rise of the Napa Valley as a preeminent wine-growing region, and its dynamic business approach heralds the future of the wine industry. 🥂

Sutter Home Fre is a sophis-ticated, sensible alternative for wine drinkers who want to enjoy the taste of a premium wine without the alcohol.

Sutter Home is America's foremost premium wine brand and an innovator in the industry, producing a full range of wines made from quality grapes grown throughout California.

Napa Wine Company

One of the oldest wineries in the Napa Valley, Napa Wine Company proudly fulfills a three-fold role within the viticultural life of the area. It is a custom crush facility for over 50 premium brands, a producer of the family's own ultra-premium brand, and a wine shop representing a rare selection of the ultra-premium wines produced at the facility. Originally built in the 1870s, the winery was purchased in 1993 by the Pelissa family, whose long-standing history of wine prompted them to renovate the facility extensively to accommodate further specialization in small-lot wine production. And the company's Oakville wine shop enables 13 of the valley's wineries to bring their products to visitors and residents alike.

The Pelissa family, current owner of the Napa Wine Company, has an extensive agricultural history. The first generation of the family emigrated from Italy in the late 19th century and began the tradition by farming grapes and other crops in the valley. Second generation farmer, Andy Pelissa was one of the Valley's viticultural pioneers and a Planning Commissioner when the Valley's landmark Agricultural Preserve was enacted. Since the family assumed leadership in 1993, the Napa Wine Company has become a leader among wine producers in the Napa Valley, with a keen interest in continuing the tradition of high-quality wine production. Andrew Hoxsey, the managing partner of the Napa Wine Company, is a member of several wine-related organizations, including the Napa Valley Vintners Association, the California Association of Wine Growers, the Napa Valley Grape Growers, the American Vineyard Foundation, and the Napa Valley Farm Bureau.

Known as one of the Valley's finest "custom crush" facilities, Napa Wine Company produces over 50 brands of wine; of these, three were judged by the Wine Spectator to be among the top wines of 1997. The renovated premium custom crush facility was designed to accommodate high quality production of small lots of wine; the size of the facility and number of tanks of multiple sizes allow wine growers to keep each lot separate until the final blend is determined. Each of the lots of crushed grapes can then be treated distinctively: for instance, their portable crush station allows them to crush lots in small sizes, crush whole clusters, and hand sort the clusters.

Though wine producers usually own their own wine-making equipment, for some it simply makes sense to use a "custom crush" facility like the Napa Wine Company. Winery equipment can be extremely capital intensive and is often not cost effective to acquire for small, boutique wine brands.

Also, larger wineries may find themselves in need of extra production space when they find they have outgrown their production capacity or are in temporary need of winery capacity because of an especially large crop.

According to Stephanie Grubbs, director of sales and marketing of the Napa Wine Company, "There are space, cost, and technological advantages for winemakers using the custom crush facility. Each wine produced here comes with its own winemaker. The skilled winemaking team provided by the Napa Wine Company, led by Rob Lawson and John McKay, oversees the treatment and processes determined by those winemakers."

The release of their own brand is the Napa Wine Company's most recent achievement. First released in March of 1999, the Napa Wine Company's 1997 Sauvignon Blanc, 1997 Pinot Blanc, and the 1996 Cabernet Sauvignon illustrate the company's wine growing philosophy: Let the vineyard do the talking.

"All grapes have distinctive flavors in the field. It is my goal to capture these flavors and marry them into world-class wines," says Randy Mason, winemaker. Their remarkable debut introduces premium wines with years of viticultural and technical experience, grapes from two of the finest grape-growing regions in Napa Valley, and a commitment to organic farming standing behind it.

Grown on 600 vineyard acres in Oakville and Yountville, the viticultural philosophy is a perpetuation of Andrew Pelissa's belief that "no one owns the land… we are all merely stewards of the soil…" Since they began farming in the valley, the Pelissa family has been growing grapes organically, without the use of chemicals. Natural techniques for removing fungus and mildew such as selective leaf and shoot removal are used in lieu of employing chemical agents. To prevent soil erosion and ensure that the land will be sustainable for years to come, "cover crops" such as grains, peas, and mustard are planted between the rows, keeping the soil full of nutrients and reducing dust. Also, the grape skins and stems that remain after crushing are composted after the harvest and added to the soil, replacing vital nutrients.

The results of this thoughtful approach can be experienced at the Napa Wine Company Wine Shop, one of the most unique and pleasurable attractions in the Napa Valley. The Oakville retail shop has the unique distinction of representing many of the most highly acclaimed wine names in one location, including of course the Napa Wine Company's own brands. All of the wines available for purchase at the store are produced on site at the Napa Wine Company's custom crush facility. The wine shop offers tastings by appointment, allowing visitors to experience the superlative quality of Napa Valley grapes refined by four generations of wine growing experience. ✿

Seguin Moreau Napa Cooperage

The coopers Seguin and Moreau formed a partnership in the late 1800s to create what is now known as Seguin Moreau, the oldest cooperage in France. For over a century, Seguin Moreau has specialized in the production of French oak wine barrels, vats, and tanks used in the production and aging of the finest wines of the world. After decades of supplying the foremost cooperage for the first growth wineries of Europe, Seguin Moreau came to the United States in the early '80s to pioneer the creation of American oak wine barrels coopered in the French tradition. For the first time, wineries that previously used American oak bourbon barrels to age wine had the opportunity to use American oak wine barrels of a quality equal to that of their French-made counterparts.

Seguin Moreau Napa Cooperage.

Combining a modern cooperage with age-old traditions, Seguin Moreau Napa Cooperage, Inc. today stands as a symbol of the art of coopering. Here visitors can watch as master coopers ply their craft to create the finest American oak wine barrels available.

The taste of an exquisite wine is a result of the marriage of flavors from the grapes themselves and the barrels that hold the wine during the aging process. More than merely a container, the oak wine barrel contributes distinctive flavors and components to the character of the wine. In the centuries-old French tradition, Seguin Moreau hand selects each oak tree used to make their barrels. Only white oak from the upper reaches of the American Midwest is used due to its slow growth and superlative aroma.

To ensure that this invaluable resource is available to future generations, Seguin Moreau is America's first cooper to fund replanting programs in the selected forests from which their oak supply is harvested.

After the oak is selected, felled, and sawn into quarters, the wood is examined and sorted according to quality, with tighter grained woods being set apart for wine. The oak is then cut and set out to age in Seguin Moreau's aging yard in Missouri for at least two years. As the wood ages, it is carefully monitored for moisture levels and tannin content. Over time, undesirable flavors fade away and leave the wood ready to be crafted into a wine barrel. The wood is then cut into staves and shipped to Seguin Moreau's Napa cooperage.

When the body of the barrel is finished, the cooper toasts it over an open fire, carmelizing the wood sugars and releasing complex and enticing aromas.

Once in the hands of the coopers, the wooden staves are selected and assembled inside a single metal hoop. As it has been for centuries, coopers use fire and water to shape the barrels as flames dance between the staves of the barrel "rose." Experience and technique guide the cooper as he controls the heat with a wet swab and stokes the fire with oak chips. Using a winch to gradually arch the staves, the cooper tightens them until the barrel is fully formed into the familiar barrel shape. Once its shape is complete, the cooper places the last metal hoops in place and the barrel is ready to be toasted.

In little fire pots all in a row, barrels are toasted over a flame to the exact degree specified by the winemaker. As the barrel is toasted, it releases a complex aroma of vanilla and spices that is later imparted to the wine as it ages in the barrel.

After the ends of the wooden staves are trimmed evenly, the barrel is fitted with heads meticulously shaped to match the grooves in the staves that hold them in place. The barrel is then assembled with all natural ingredients, wooden dowels, river reed and wheat flour paste. After the heads are fitted, the final hoops are set in place.

As the last step, the barrel is checked for tightness. The cooper fills the barrels with near boiling water and adds air, while rocking the barrel back and forth vigorously. Any leaks become apparent immediately. Any imperfections of the wood are repaired and the process is repeated until the cooper is certain the barrel is completely watertight. At last the barrel is planed, scraped, and sanded to show off the fine quality of the oak, and when the last hoops are finally set in place, the cooper signs his name as coopers have done for generations before.

Thanks to the research and work done by Seguin Moreau under the direction of Alain Fouquet, a fourth-generation master cooper and

The master coopers at Seguin Moreau craft barrels with American oak according to traditional French methods.

president of Seguin Moreau's U.S. operations, Seguin Moreau blends prestigious French tradition, American resources, and a dedication to fine barrel making that erases all boundaries. Today, Seguin Moreau's superior quality American oak wine barrels have taken their place next to French oak barrels and are being used worldwide in the making of world-class wines. 🍷

During the barrel-making process, the wooden staves are heated over an open fire and dampened with water in order to gently bend the staves.

Robert Mondavi

Robert Mondavi is more than a preeminent wine producer; under the direction of the talented members of the Robert Mondavi family, the company is committed to advancing California's wine industry and the enhancement of their community by creating lasting institutions to benefit the area. A guiding force in the Napa Valley, Robert Mondavi produces a world-class family of wines and remains a strong unparalleled leader in the industry.

The Robert Mondavi Winery was a family venture from its very inception; even today, all the members of the family participate in the company. The winery was founded in 1966 by Robert G. Mondavi with his son Michael; Robert's son Timothy and daughter Marcia soon joined the team. Today Robert Mondavi continues to act as chairman of the board, while Michael Mondavi serves as president and CEO of the winery, Timothy is managing director and winegrower, and Marcia is a director of the company. Margrit Biever, Robert's wife, currently serves as vice president of cultural affairs at the winery and has been instrumental in shaping the Robert Mondavi Winery culinary and cultural programs.

The Robert Mondavi family of wines is international in scope: celebrating the wine-growing traditions of California, Italy, and France, the portfolio of wines includes numerous prestigious labels. Best known is Robert Mondavi Winery in Oakville, the first in the family and long recognized as an innovator in the industry and a producer of world class wines. In addition to its To-kalon Vineyard in Oakville, the winery also owns vineyards in the Stags Leap and Carneros Districts of

Napa. Woodbridge Winery, acquired in 1979, is one of the largest and most modern wineries in the world, and uses many of the same traditional methods as the Napa Valley winery. Opus One, produced in Oakville, is the result of Robert Mondavi's partnership with Baroness Philippine de Rothschild of Chateau Mouton Rothschild in France. A celebration of two cultures, Opus One is an ultra premium Bordeaux-style red wine. Other wines in the

The Robert Mondavi Winery, Oakville.

Robert Mondavi family of wines include Robert Mondavi Coastal, produced from grapes grown on California's North and Central coasts; La Famiglia di Robert Mondavi, a celebration of the family's roots in northern Italy, producing traditional wines such as Barbera, Sangiovese, and Pinot Grigio in the Napa Valley; Caliterra, a joint venture between Mondavi and the Eduardo Chadwick family of Chile; Byron Vineyard & Winery; Vichon Mediterranean; and Luce, a joint venture with the Frescobaldi family of Florence, Italy.

An important part of Robert Mondavi's contribution to the life of the valley is the company's commitment to creating lasting institutions that benefit the community. The winery has sponsored art exhibitions, seminars on viticultural concerns, and boasts the most comprehensive winery tour program in the valley. The Summer Music Festival at Robert Mondavi Winery brings enthusiastic audiences to the valley every year, and the winery also hosts the Great Chefs at the Robert Mondavi Winery. 🐝

Timothy Mondavi, managing director and winegrower; Michael Mondavi, president and CEO; and Robert Mondavi, founder and chairman of the board.

Clos Du Val Wine Co., Ltd.

In 1970, Clos Du Val owner and founder John Goelet came to Bernard Portet and asked his help in selecting the perfect piece of land to create a vineyard. Portet, who had been raised in the Bordeaux region of France and trained in both agronomy and winemaking, then traveled the world for two years, visiting nearly every wine-growing country in the world. The selection was Napa Valley.

What distinguishes Clos Du Val from many wineries is that from the start the terroir—the combination of soil and climate—in which they chose to plant, was selected specifically to grow Bordeaux type grapes. Portet eventually chose a parcel of land in what would be designated as the Stags Leap District, since recognized as the preeminent wine-producing district in the Napa Valley.

"We knew what we wanted to grow, and we selected the area according to what we wanted to grow. At the time, that was not at all the concept here," says Portet. Most of the crushed grapes were produced by independent growers, with very little communication between the winemaker and the grape grower. "I offered our French school of thought, that grape growing and wine making are intimately linked. I was looking at growing the best grapes possible to make the best wines possible."

Clos Du Val's vineyards supply 80 percent of the grapes the winery crushes, allowing the winemakers to ensure the utmost quality of the fruit. The wine making team at Clos Du Val, augmented in recent years, brings together individuals with a wide range of experiences: Bernard Portet, President and Winemaker, studied winemaking at Montpellier; John Clews, Director of Winery Operations, is also a winemaker whose forte is Chardonnay and Pinot Noir; and Kian Tavakoli, Associate Winemaker, specializes in Bordeaux style wines. Clews and Tavakoli both earned degrees from the University of California—Davis.

Clos Du Val's wine making team: (from left to right) Bernard Portet, President and Winemaker; John Clews, Director of Winery Operations; and Kian Tavakoli, Associate Winemaker.

The combination of a classical wine making style with the fine terroir of the Napa Valley has proved eminently successful: In 1986, Clos Du Val took First Place in the remake of the famous January 1976 Paris tasting, placing above several prominent Bordeaux chateaux; and more recently, the Clos Du Val 1987 Reserve Cabernet Sauvignon won the Trophy in the 1994 annual competition of the Association of French Enologists. "For me, it's very encouraging to see that we are on the right track, that our wines are of an international level of quality, and that people, whether in the United States or Europe, really appreciate the style of wine that we are developing," says Portet.

Clos Du Val sponsors Chamber Music in Napa Valley and the Napa Valley Wine Auction. Portet served as the auction chair in 1997 and belongs to the Wine Institute, the Napa Valley Vintners Association, the American Society for Enology and Viticulture, and the Wine Service Co-op. ❧

Clos Du Val's facility in the Stags Leap District of the Napa Valley.

Chalone Wine Group

Chalone Wine Group owns and operates a group of six prestigious wineries, including Acacia Winery in the Carneros District of the Napa Valley. Under the direction of its new CEO Tom Selfridge, Chalone Wine Group is celebrating record sales and the promise of more good fortune to come; Selfridge comes to Chalone Wine Group after holding executive positions at Beaulieu and Kendall-Jackson Wineries. The Napa-based company, founded in 1972, also supports the Chalone Wine Foundation, a non-profit organization dedicated to administering the company's charitable interests.

Acacia Winery, founded in 1979, is the second-oldest winery in the renowned Carneros region and the Napa Valley representative in the Chalone Wine Group's portfolio of wineries. One of the outstanding wine producers in California, Acacia is well known for its pinot noir; the cooler climate of the Carneros region is ideal for growing Bordeaux-style grapes, and Acacia's Pinot Noir is produced in the traditional French style. Acacia Winery also makes chardonnay, its principal wine, and produces small amounts of brut and viognier as well.

Other wineries in the Chalone Wine Group include Chalone Vineyard in Monterey County, Edna Valley Vineyard in San Luis Obispo; Carmenet Vineyard in Sonoma; Canoe Ridge Vineyard in Walla Walla, Washington; and Chateau Duhart-Milon in the Bordeaux region of France. Also, Chalone Wine Group recently released a new label, Echelon, an intriguing blend of grapes from several of the company's vineyards; the new brand represents Chalone Wine Group's commitment to innovation and the promise of future growth for the company.

Seeking to give something back to the community which made its success possible, the Chalone Wine Group established the Chalone Wine Foundation, a non-profit organization which oversees the Chalone Wine Group's charitable activities. The Chalone Wine Foundation provides grants to nonprofit organizations through its participation in the Napa Valley Community Foundation, and supports local activities with wine donations. "We're very community-oriented and feel strongly about demonstrating that through the Foundation," says W. Philip Woodward, president of the Chalone Wine Foundation and chairman and co-founder of the Chalone Wine Group. "We try to concentrate on programs that create jobs for people who live in Napa County, especially in the food and wine industry." Proceeds from the Chalone Wine Group's Annual Shareholder Celebration benefit the Richard H. Graff Scholarship Fund, established in honor of Chalone Wine Group co-founder Dick Graff, which provides financial assistance to students interested in studying food and wine.

Chalone Wine Group is a publicly held company listed on the NASDAQ stock exchange; shareholders enjoy special benefits including special wine offerings, tours, and events, as well as the knowledge that they are benefiting the community by their involvement in the Chalone Wine Foundation. The Chalone Wine Group employs approximately forty-five people at its headquarters in Napa's Gateway Business Park, which oversees sales, administration, financial and accounting activities, warehousing, and shipping for all of the company's wineries. ❧

Chalone Wine Group owns and operates Acacia Winery in the Carneros District of the Napa Valley, well known for its chardonnay and pinot noir.

Chalone Wine Group moved its headquarters to Napa's Gateway Business Park in 1993.

Wine Country Cases Inc.

In 1988, Wine Country Cases co-founders Dan Pina and Ignacio Delgadillo were employed at a small winery as production manager and cellarmaster respectively. The winery had been using wooden wine boxes made by a company which was becoming too large to service both their winery and the other wineries that had gotten them started in the first place. Pina and Delgadillo saw a business opportunity: "Basically the small wineries which got them started were now being told, 'If you can't use this many, then we can't make the boxes.' So we figured all these customers that they were disregarding would be a place to start," says Pina.

He and Delgadillo rented a small facility in Calistoga where they set up shop and began making boxes in their spare time. The partners built much of the equipment they started using, rebuilding old fruit packing machines from the 1950s to suit their needs. "For about the first six months, all we did was build equipment," says Pina. The two had been making small wooden bungs for wine barrels previously; however, learning their new trade and perfecting their technique took some time. "The first order we made took us about two and a half months, now it takes about four days… it was a very slow process."

In 1996, Wine Country Cases moved from its 2,000-square-foot space in Calistoga to its present 10,000-square-foot facility in St. Helena. "We were able to build a building with our production needs taken care of," says Pina. "We ended up with a facility that allows us to serve large and small clients alike. Now we generally won't refuse anyone: there's no order too small or too big."

Approximately 75 percent of Wine Country Cases' business is wine-related. "We make anything that a wine bottle will fit in," states Pina. All production is done at their St. Helena facility, where they employ around 30 people. In addition to assembling the cases, they decorate them with winery logos by branding the design into the soft wood, often adding double-exposed designs and colored foil accents. Gift boxes, displays, and point of sale items are also designed and manufactured at the St. Helena facility.

Wine Country Cases supplies over 50 varieties of boxes for packaging wine and food to wineries and retailers all over the United States; however, most of the company's business originates in the Napa Valley. "We are fortunate to be able to make premium wood packaging that compliments all of the premium wines and food products that are produced around us," says Pina.

Wine Country Cases' St. Helena facility. The company supplies fine wooden boxes to wineries throughout the Napa Valley.

All aspects of production, from assembly to decoration, are performed in house at the 10,000-square-foot facility.

The Barrel Shop

The Barrel Shop sits on the busy thoroughfare of Highway 29, south of Napa in American Canyon; driving by the shop, tourists and residents alike slow down to take a look at the garden of objects sitting outside. Owner Ron Young, who began his career as a cooper in Missouri, uses both his own creative inclinations and the inspiration of his customers to create anything and everything out of barrels.

Among the most popular items at the Barrel Shop are Young's patented wine racks. Available in two different styles, the wine racks are crafted completely out of recycled barrels. The full cask wine rack, which holds twenty-eight bottles of wine, is crafted from an entire wine barrel; a few of the staves are removed to create an opening, then the shelves, which are made from the extra staves, are fitted inside the barrel. The whole wine rack rests on casters for easy maneuvering and is available with or without doors. A second style is the countertop wine rack, which holds twenty bottles of wine. Easy to transport and ideal for locations with limited space, the countertop wine rack is made from the midsection of a wine barrel which is set on its side and fitted with shelves inside the circle. Both styles of wine racks are crafted wholly out of used barrels; no outside wood is used, and even the scrap wood is utilized for toasting material.

Ron Young displays one of his creations, a full cask wine rack.

The small wine barrels that Young creates from previously used barrels are among the most useful and unique items available at the Barrel Shop. The refurbished barrels are ideal for the home winemaker; because the wood from the barrels has already been used for wine, it lacks the harsh flavor of new oak, but furnishes all of the oak flavor a home winemaker needs. The staves are removed from the larger barrels, sized down, and sanded to smoothness to create barrels that range in size from five liters to thirty gallons. The small wine barrels allow amateur winemakers to age their wine longer without worrying about harsh oak taste and achieve a more complex flavor.

Young opened the Barrel Shop in 1991, looking for fresh challenges when his job as a cooper brought him to California; now another enterprise begins a new chapter for the artisan. Young and partner Mike Martin are merging officially at the beginning of the new millennium; Martin's current business, Hollow Oak, specializes in wholesale lawn and garden crafts made from recycled wine barrels. Currently the Barrel Shop has customers worldwide, from locations throughout the United States to Japan and Korea. Young and Martin's new association will enable them to combine their resources and expand production of the small barrels, wine racks, and other items crafted from the unique containers of Napa Valley's wine industry. 🜲

Mike Martin with one of his newest creations, a table top fountain produced from a 10 liter wine barrel.

Workers are overshadowed by huge holding tanks at Clos Du Val Winery in Napa.

CHAPTER 6

Hospitality, Attractions, and the Marketplace

Jimmy Vasser Chevrolet Toyota

Jimmy Vasser's track record as an award-winning Indy-Car driver has been consistently outstanding, and Jimmy's most recent endeavor in the world of cars and driving is no exception. Since its grand opening in 1998, Jimmy Vasser Chevrolet Toyota has proved that a unique combination of excellent service, devotion to customers, and a love of driving is a sure winner.

Jimmy's racing career and champion status provide an exciting theme and a major draw for the public at the dealership located on Soscol. The showroom is a standout with its race-themed neon signs, vintage soda fountain counter, and an ice cream freezer fully stocked with cones for customers of every age. In the dealership's boutique, customers can browse through all kinds of racing merchandise from jackets to models of Jimmy's Indy-Car while placing an order with the parts department.

What fuels its ever-increasing popularity is the Vasser commitment to rapport with the customers, its highest priority. Customers are interested in not only a quality car but also a long-term relationship with a company that wants to grow with the Napa community. A strong sales staff makes this possible. When Jimmy Vasser bought the dealership in May of 1998, no major staff changes were made, and, in fact, the employee count has increased since then. Sales personnel have the benefit of three-day training courses, and the dealership furnishes in-house training every week.

It all comes down to strong community ties: establishing relationships with their customers and sharing the benefits of their success. Jimmy Vasser Chevrolet Toyota donates generously to charities in the Napa Valley. For every car sold during their grand opening, the dealership donated money to the local Boys and Girls Club, and the proceeds from the parts department were given to Vine Village, a facility for challenged individuals. The dealership's support of the Chamber of Commerce's Toys for Tots event helped bring in nine barrels of new toys for local children.

Looking toward the future, Darren Smyl, Partner/General Manager, anticipates that business will continue to grow rapidly thanks to their new web sites, which promise to be another vehicle for their commitment to excellent customer service. Shoppers can buy a car, order parts, book an appointment, or ask questions about maintenance over the Internet. Customers who request information or post questions via e-mail can expect a response within five hours. By doing their research at home, customers have time to relax, enjoy the dealership's casual atmosphere, and feel that they are not only buying a car but also establishing a solid relationship with a progressive business that will take care of their needs long into the future. ☙

Flags wave cheerfully over the wide selection of vehicles at Jimmy Vasser's lot on Napa's busy auto row.

The retro 50s-themed showroom at Jimmy Vasser Chevrolet Toyota is frequently host to rare and classic cars.

The Yountville Inn

If you're looking for superior accommodations in one of the world's loveliest areas, The Yountville Inn is a rare find for a traveler visiting the Napa Valley. The Inn blends comfort with the casual elegance of the Napa Valley, offering a convenient home base for exploring the wine country. Newly opened in the summer of 1998, The Yountville Inn offers its guests ideal lodging for a Napa Valley getaway.

Situated at the southern tip of Yountville, just east of Highway 29's lovely stretch up-valley, the family-owned inn is a short walk from fine dining and shopping in Yountville's historic downtown area. It is ideally located for a jaunt up the valley to world-renowned wineries and restaurants that are just minutes away. The Inn is also adjacent to the Yountville Golf Course and the Veterans' Park, with its bocci ball and sand volleyball courts. The green hills of the valley slope to either side of the town, while the historic blackberry-strewn Hopper Creek runs alongside The Yountville Inn.

Walking into the Italian-tiled reception area, visitors will feel immediately at ease in the Inn's comfortable and relaxing ambiance. A graceful stone archway over the front desk graces the flower-adorned foyer. Slate, wood, and stone surfaces are plentiful and delightful to the eye, from the fieldstone fireplaces in each room to the high vaulted ceilings of the Club Room. The natural fibers and textures of the Inn's custom furnishings complement the stone-and-wood architecture and echo back to the natural beauty of the Napa Valley.

Tired travelers can take a dip in the heated swimming pool or relax in the spa under a cool evening sky while enjoying the clean country air. Each guest will find the rooms to be the height of comfort. The fireplaces found in every room are perfect for lounging with

Comfortable and versatile executive conference facilities can accommodate from six to sixty people, and will help make any meeting successful.

loved ones, and charming pine armoires each hold a large screen TV and VCR. Additional amenities include a hairdryer, iron and ironing board, refrigerator, coffee maker, and plush terry velour robes. The Inn offers a tempting complimentary continental breakfast in its pleasant lobby every morning.

For the business person looking for a unique location to hold a special meeting or retreat, the Yountville Inn has executive conference facilities that can accommodate from six to sixty people. And the Club Room, which is also perfect for a casual meeting place, offers a sunny, cozy place to munch on a scone and enjoy fresh gourmet coffee before heading up on a winery tour. From their entrance through the lovely French doors to the moment they step back out into the clear morning sunshine, guests will find The Yountville Inn a luxurious place to savor the Napa Valley's many pleasures.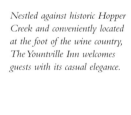

Nestled against historic Hopper Creek and conveniently located at the foot of the wine country, The Yountville Inn welcomes guests with its casual elegance.

Napa Valley Exposition

Since the early 1860s, the fairgrounds in Napa has been hosting the colorful activities that reflect the town's true character. From the weekend crab feeds in winter to the Town and Country Fair in summer, the fairgrounds at Napa Valley Expo provide "an interactive experience where people come together to celebrate the uniqueness of the Napa Valley." That's the enthusiastic sentiment of Dorothy Lind, CEO of the Napa Valley Expo since 1989.

The Town and Country Fair celebrated each August originated from early traveling road shows called *chautauquas*. Today the Fair remains a bastion of American creativity and individual excellence. "The remarkable artwork, baked goods, amazing quilts, and other homemade creations celebrate the community connection that we have in the exhibit program, and is the most important part of the Fair," Dorothy is proud to say. Over 13,000 entries compete for recognition, more than in any other Fair of its size in California.

The Expo hosts special events all year long raising money for general nonprofit organizations valleywide. The Expo's budget is about $1 million, but it manages to raise easily one and a half times that amount. Political debates, trade shows, concerts, the Spring Fair that showcases the talents of local schoolchildren, Bingo, Grad Night, and celebrity galas take their turn in the Expo's popular buildings: Cabernet, Merlot, Riesling, and the largest, Chardonnay, which is booked a year in advance.

With the passage of Senate Bill 1436 in 1998, Napa Valley Expo became the first fairground in California to return to local management since the state assumed control of most Fairs in the 1930s when horse racing was legalized. Because of its prime location, the Expo is an important part of the renaissance in downtown Napa. Public forums are a major factor in deciding how the fairgrounds' 35 acres will blend with commercial use to complete Napa's restoration to a vibrant Victorian river city. A conference center and hotel are envisioned, along with a teaching farm. A collection of 66 classic horse-drawn carriages donated to the Expo by George Geis may tour the streets of downtown Napa, linking its envisioned future to its treasured past.

"The Expo serves as a catalyst for community vision for the Napa Valley," Dorothy Lind says. Symbolizing the Expo's role in cooperative problem solving, is a huge round table in the Director's House that was specially constructed to be available to nonprofits and local and state government as a gesture of the Expo's desire to help determine a sustainable future for the entire Napa Valley. The round table seats twenty and is often the setting for creative compromise. "A circle joins everyone together," as Dorothy points out, "and the Napa Valley Expo exists to do exactly that." ☙

The annual Fair is fun for everyone.

RiverPointe Napa Valley

Just upriver from the explosion of development in downtown Napa, RiverPointe Napa Valley is the area's newest five-star resort. It presents an exciting option for visitors to the Valley who are dismayed by the often-difficult task of finding accommodations. The Napa Valley hosts millions of visitors during the year, yet there are comparatively few rooms available to meet the demand; the scarcity of hotels and the often steep prices may preclude visitors from extending their stay in the Valley beyond one day. Just minutes from downtown Napa, RiverPointe Napa Valley offers Vacation Ownership, an exciting alternative to the typical all-suite hotel.

RiverPointe Napa Valley gives visitors the opportunity to do more than briefly taste the Valley's many exciting features. Vacation Ownership enables them to experience the wine country lifestyle, allowing the time and the security to explore the area at a leisurely pace while living in comfortable, homey surroundings. Owning vacation time in the Valley enables guests to feel more a part of the community rather than just a weekend tourist. RiverPointe's Wine Country Cottages are specifically designed to reflect the Valley's casual elegance, featuring large sunny windows, fully-equipped kitchens, and private decks. The clubhouse offers an exercise center, an events room, and other facilities for guests' use. Members also receive discounts at participating restaurants and stores throughout the Valley. Because RiverPointe Napa Valley is a vacation ownership club and an affiliate of Interval International, membership also entitles owners to exchange time in Napa for time at any of Interval's hundreds of resorts worldwide.

RiverPointe Napa Valley is an attractive option for those who value repeated and more relaxed visits to this world-famous area. Another advantage of membership at RiverPointe Napa Valley is the benefit of their day-use program, which enables members to use the club's outdoor swimming pool and spa with picnic and barbecue area whenever they are in town. Timesharing is vacation planning for the moment and for the future.

RiverPointe Napa Valley anticipates a total membership of six to seven thousand families. With the redevelopment proceeding in downtown Napa, the new Napa Valley Expo, the American Center for Wine, Food and the Arts, and the work being done on the Napa River, Napa is an exciting place to be. With thousands of people visiting the Valley each year, RiverPointe members are welcomed by the local community because of the stability of the resort and its positive economic impact. ☙

The American Center for Wine, Food and the Arts

The design for the new American Center for Wine, Food and the Arts includes a variety of facilities—museum galleries, an auditorium, a café restaurant, a gift shop, a concert terrace, state-of-the-art teaching kitchens and classrooms, and 3 1/2 acres of gardens—yet the ambitious project is indeed even more than the sum of its parts. As a cultural museum and educational destination, the Center will host activities and exhibits that explore American culture. By integrating the Napa Valley's affinity for fine food, wines, viticulture, agriculture, and art in one facility, the Center will also enrich and define the unique interplay of all these components, becoming yet another prized element in the experience of wine country.

The American Center for Wine, Food and the Arts is a nonprofit organization dedicated to exploring the distinctively American approach to wine, food, and the arts. Visitors to the Center can tailor their experience to suit their interests, whether by attending a musical performance, taking a cooking class, watching a demonstration by a guest chef, attending a wine tasting class, or visiting the exhibition spaces. "Our plan is to provide a variety of different options and an exceptional experience for each visitor to the American Center," says Peggy Loar, director.

With so many activity options in the ever-changing menu of programs, guests will find something to enrich their visit. "We will challenge our visitors' expectations. We plan to feature sculpture, installations, videoart, and crafts that touch on the subject matter of wine and food in surprising and intriguing ways," says Betty Teller, assistant director for exhibitions. In addition to such adult activities as wine tasting classes, the Center will also offer children's programs, including art, cooking, and garden classes centered around a seasonal outdoor kitchen.

The vision of the American Center for Wine, Food and the Arts began 10 years ago as the dream of Robert Mondavi; he originally envisioned the Center as an educational facility for professionals in the viticultural field. Gradually Mondavi began to conceive of the project as a cultural center and as an asset to the cultural life of Northern California. As a part of the commitment he has shown to revitalizing the city of Napa, he helped the Center purchase 12 acres on the oxbow of the Napa River in 1996.

Your experience at the American Center begins when you park in a garden setting and make your way to the entrance placed at the end of a beautiful path.

The most recent addition to the explosion of activity in the city of Napa, the American Center for Wine, Food and the Arts already boasts a large pre-debut membership. "Every year we host a series of public programs through our annual Festival of Olives. We want to give the community a sense of the excitement that the Center will generate once it opens," says Daphne Derven, Curator. A national center celebrating wine and food in a beautiful valley renowned for its wineries and fine cuisine, the American Center for Wine, Food and the Arts promises to be a resource for the community that will enthrall and edify its visitors. 🍇

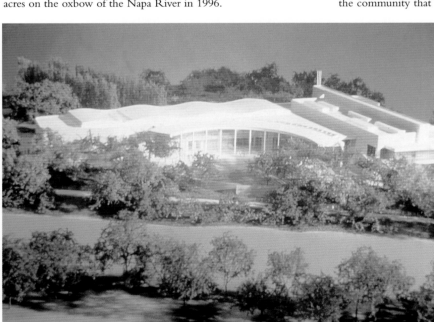

The outdoor concert terrace provides casual seating for over 500 guests to enjoy musical and theatrical performances on the banks of the Napa River.

Patrons at Beringer Wine Estates enjoy a wine-tasting party.

CHAPTER 7

Health Care &
Education

Queen of the Valley Hospital

This Catholic not-for-profit, full-service, 166-bed hospital is the major diagnostic and therapeutic medical center for the Napa Valley and surrounding region. With its reputation for excellence and its unwavering commitment to meeting local needs, Queen of the Valley Hospital is a cherished and vital member of the Napa community.

From its inception, Queen of the Valley Hospital was a labor of love. It began quietly as a dream of the Sisters of St. Joseph of Orange, who were acutely aware of the inadequacies of post-war health care in the Napa area. Assuming leadership of the former Parks Victory Hospital on Jefferson Street on May 1, 1953, the Sisters were determined to create a new facility for the Napa community within a mere five years. True to their resolve, the Sisters opened the new Queen of the Valley Hospital on March 5, 1958, at its present location at 1000 Trancas Street. The Queen, as Queen of the Valley Hospital is often referred to with affection, was made possible by combining the Sisters' vision and mission of caregiving with the support and fundraising expertise of Napa's dedicated civic leaders. This relationship has continued through the years and has brought Queen of the Valley Hospital into a new era of health care.

Forty years of careful planning have seen the hospital and its reputation grow along with the community. Thanks to the high

Queen of the Valley Hospital has been caring for the people of the Napa Valley for more than 40 years.

expectations of Napa Valley residents, the range of advanced specialty services available at Queen of the Valley is comparable in quality and scope to those offered by university and urban-based hospitals, and its accreditation ratings are as high or higher than those of major Bay Area teaching hospitals. Queen of the Valley Hospital offers the area's only neonatal intensive care unit, community cancer

Queen of the Valley Hospital serves as the state-designated Trauma Center for Napa County.

Certified therapy dogs are another tool to help patients undergoing rehabilitation therapy regain their functioning.

medicine, computerized tomography (CT) scans, and magnetic resonance imaging (MRI). The Breast Center offers self-care programs, consultations, and mammography examinations. State-of-the-art stereotactic detection, a more comfortable alternative to surgical biopsy, is available if necessary.

Queen of the Valley Hospital's Home Care Services ensures a smooth transition from the hospital to home, allowing patients to recuperate from surgery or illnesses in the comfort of their own surroundings. Nurses, home health aides, therapists, social workers, and chaplains work together to provide patients with the coordinated, physician-prescribed care they need for a successful recovery.

The Acute Rehabilitation Center at Queen of the Valley Hospital is the only facility of its kind in the region. The unit provides comprehensive physical, occupational, and speech therapy for those who have experienced a major stroke or

center, and acute rehabilitation center, not to mention one of the region's finest heart centers and women's health care centers.

Most of the 200-plus physicians who practice at the Queen are members of Napa Valley Physicians, an independent practice association. Nearly three out of four Napa Valley residents are cared for by a Napa Valley Physicians member associated with Queen of the Valley Hospital. Representing nearly 50 medical specialties, Napa Valley Physicians offers ready access to care and the kind of one-on-one, long-term patient/physician relationships that promote high-quality care and ensure patient satisfaction.

As the state-designated trauma center for Napa County, Queen of the Valley Hospital's specially trained Trauma Team is ready day and night to care for victims of accidents and other traumas. The Emergency Department is open 24 hours a day and a landing pad for medical helicopters is conveniently located just outside the Emergency Room doors. In addition, *Express*Care at Queen of the Valley Hospital offers a

trauma. Eighty percent of the patients in acute rehabilitation are older adults recovering from strokes, but the center also cares for victims of brain and spinal cord injuries, fractures, amputations, burns, and neurological disorders. In addition, a Transitional Rehabilitation Center operates as a short-term skilled nursing facility for the hospital and cares for patients with significant problems that may be dealt with in one to two weeks. Patients who stay in these centers also get the opportunity to benefit from the "healing paws" and affections of the certified therapy dogs who visit regularly.

The Queen's Intensive Care Nursery allows premature and sick babies to be treated in their own community.

perfect option for tourists, visitors, and others without a local physician or in need of after-hours urgent care.

One of the hospital's most distinguished specialty services is its Regional Heart Center, which offers outstanding care and a full complement of services, from EKG monitoring and angioplasty to complex open heart surgery and cardiac rehabilitation. A comprehensive Cardiac Catheterization Lab is fully equipped to perform advanced diagnostic tests and interventional procedures.

The Queen's Community Cancer Center, approved by the Commission on Cancer, specializes in patient-focused care. Complete diagnostic imaging services include ultrasound, nuclear

Maternal and Child Health Services offers a wide array of birth experience options for women and their families, as well as classes on prenatal care, childbirth, breastfeeding, and sibling participation. The area's only Intensive Care Nursery (ICN) provides expert and loving care for premature and high-risk infants. Situated right in the middle of the Maternity Center, the ICN is important to Napa Valley residents because it allows babies to be cared for in this community with their parents nearby. It provides high-quality care and enormous peace of mind. The same holds true for the sick children who are cared for in the Queen's Pediatric Unit, the only dedicated Pediatric Unit in the Valley.

Over the years, there have been significant changes at Queen of the Valley Hospital, including the addition of two new wings, a nursing pavilion, the Community Cancer Center, a brand new Emergency Department, and expansion of the Intensive Care Unit. What hasn't changed is the Sisters' personal approach to the healing mission of Christ. As part of St. Joseph Health System, sponsored by the Sisters of St. Joseph of Orange, the hospital remains guided by four core values: Dignity, Service, Excellence, and Justice. To this day, infusing the activities of every aspect of care at Queen of the Valley Hospital is a commitment to these values:

• Dignity: We respect each person as an inherently valuable member of the human community and as a unique expression of life.

• Service: We bring together people who recognize that every interaction is a unique opportunity to serve one another, the community, and society.

• Excellence: We foster personal and professional development, accountability, innovation, teamwork, and commitment to quality.

• Justice: We advocate for systems and structures that are attuned to the needs of the vulnerable and disadvantaged and that promote a sense of community among all persons.

"Helping to heal all we touch" is the mission of Queen of the Valley Hospital. According to Sister Patricia Haley, Vice President of Sponsorship, "The hospital exemplifies our mission and values internally by providing the highest quality medical care to patients; we carry our mission and values out into the community by partnering with other entities in ways that improve our community's health. As the largest non-governmental employer and the most comprehensive health care facility

While many hospitals place children on adult patient floors, the Queen is the only hospital in the Valley with a dedicated Pediatric Unit.

in the area, Queen of the Valley Hospital feels a strong responsibility to be a community 'partner.'"

From the beginning, Queen of the Valley Hospital has been committed to extending its role in the community far beyond the traditional medical model to address such public health concerns as domestic violence, medical and dental services for low-income families, prenatal care, quality child care, health education, and much more. The hospital's outreach to the underserved has blossomed thanks to community-wide collaboration between the hospital and Napa County, the Napa Valley Coalition of Non-profit Agencies, and the area's businesses and churches.

Among the many local, community-based programs that have been enhanced by the participation and funding of the hospital's Health Care for the Poor Committee are: Community Health Clinic Ole, a primary care provider for indigent and uninsured individuals and families; Healthy Moms & Babies, a collaborative effort providing a seamless system of maternity services in the Napa Valley for low-income women; COPE (Child or Parent Emergency), which provides a number of services (many bilingual) to reduce the stress of parenting and teach parents critical parenting skills; Los Niños Child Development and Family Program, which provides high-quality child care to low-income families; and Nuestra Esperanza, a multipurpose center for Latinos who have been separated from the community by language and cultural barriers.

Partnering with community organizations, such as Los Niños Child Development and Family Program, is part of how the Queen helps to build a healthy community.

Adult Day Services of Napa Valley offers comprehensive health care, rehabilitative therapies, social services, and personal care for frail, elderly persons and younger functionally impaired adults.

utmost in privacy and comfort, a new bi-plane catheterization laboratory for the Regional Heart Center, brachytherapy to concentrate prostate cancer treatment in the affected areas, and a multileaf collimator to enhance breast cancer radiation treatments.

With its strong personal connection to the community and the ability to deliver superior medical care with the latest technologies, Queen of the Valley Hospital continues to attract dedicated physicians and staff of the highest caliber. Working together, the men and women of this hospital reach out to those in need with love and concern to help heal the whole person—body, mind, and spirit. Thanks to Queen of the Valley's personal approach, trained personnel and state-of-the-art facilities, residents will always be assured of receiving high-quality care close to home. ☺

Hospice of Napa Valley and its Adult Day Services programs are joint projects of Queen of the Valley and St. Helena Hospitals that provide home and facility-based care for the terminally ill, and therapies and social activities for frail, elderly persons and functionally impaired adults. Through its wide variety of ongoing programs, support groups, senior health education classes, and special lectures and events for the public, Queen of the Valley invites the community to take advantage of the many resources the hospital offers.

Most new construction and equipment purchases for the hospital are made possible by the Queen of the Valley Hospital Foundation, which enjoys a broad base of community support. Major gifts and planned giving raise about $1 million annually for special projects for the hospital, and endowments now amount to well over $4 million. Special events that receive generous and enthusiastic community participation include the Reach for the Stars cancer survivors' brunch and fashion show and the Day for the Queen festivities. By the end of 1998, the Foundation successfully completed its $950,000 fundraising project for a new peripheral vascular laboratory. Through their support of the hospital foundation, it's clear that residents of this Valley are eager to participate in building a healthy tomorrow for themselves, their families, and their community.

The next challenges on the horizon for the Foundation and Queen of the Valley Hospital are planning for an expanded birth center to allow the

The new bi-plane cardiac catherization lab provides cardiologists and surgeons with state-of-the-art technology for diagnosis and treatment of heart disorders.

DEY

Asthma's debilitating symptoms affect approximately 17 million people in the United States, and asthma is the most common childhood disease in this country. What's more, the number of people suffering from the wheezing and breathlessness of this disease increases each year.

That's the bad news. The good news is that advanced pharmacological medications are being developed to help people better manage their asthma.

Napa Valley is fortunate to be the home of DEY, a specialty pharmaceutical company creating innovative, high-tech solutions to respiratory problems. Now, DEY is developing unique new delivery systems and novel drug formulations to treat respiratory diseases even more effectively in the future.

DEY, a subsidiary of Merck KGaA of Darmstadt, Germany, develops, manufactures, and sells respiratory products for the treatment of asthma, bronchitis, and chronic obstructive pulmonary disease (COPD).

Founded in 1978, DEY is a leading supplier to physicians, pharmacists, retail drug stores, managed-care providers, and hospitals. DEY is also among the world's largest manufacturers of specialty unit-dose inhalation medications that provide a cost-effective means of relief to persons suffering from asthma and chronic lung diseases.

Located in the Corporate Park at the southern tip of the Valley, DEY has a lovely view of green hills and old oaks. But despite the

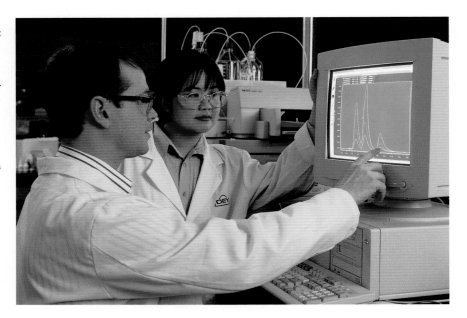

pastoral setting, the facility is a high-tech haven for all aspects of the pharmaceutical business: the administrative offices, sales and marketing group, research and development laboratories, and manufacturing are all here. One of the earliest tenants in the Corporate Park in 1987, DEY is a vital part of the county's thriving economic community.

DEY is one of the largest private employers in the county, with over 600 employees at its Napa location. "Most people don't realize there is a major pharmaceutical company right here in the Valley, but the location has worked well for the company and its employees," says Robert F. Mozak, Executive Vice President of sales and marketing at DEY. Mozak is on the Board of Directors of the Napa Chamber of Commerce, and DEY has been the

An excellent staff, from researchers to technicians, strives to uphold the exacting standards that are the DEY hallmark.

Every step of the way, DEY emphasizes product quality and consistency and is dedicated to meeting customers' needs.

major sponsor of the Napa River Festival, providing a major portion of funding for this community celebration over the past several years.

DEY is growing at an astonishing rate: sales have grown at least 20 percent each of the past eight years, and Mozak anticipates the same kind of growth in the future. The company's goal of releasing at least two new products each year for the next several years, as well as a focus on future technological developments, are further proof of this fast-growing company's strength.

Though the wine business and tourist trade are usually synonymous in this winery-rich region, DEY represents the alternate side of Napa Valley's economic vigor. The growing demand for solutions to respiratory illnesses represents both a challenge and an opportunity for the company to excel. Never resting on past successes, the men and women of DEY continue to develop a wide range of exciting products in the field of respiratory care. With global resources and a firm commitment to providing respiratory care products that are both affordable and easy to use, DEY looks forward to a prosperous future—right here in Napa Valley. ☙

The use of advanced technology such as this aseptic manufacturing equipment assures the DEY reputation for unsurpassed quality.

Santen Incorporated

Santen, in Chinese, means to act with the sanction of heaven. In that spirit, Santen has contributed to eye care, in all areas throughout the world, to ensure better vision and better health for a brighter future for all people. Santen understands the beauty of vision and has been committed to protecting the joy of sight for over 100 years. Founded in 1890, in Osaka, Japan, Santen is the oldest ethical ophthalmic company in the world today, built on the promise to contribute to society by providing products that improve the quality of life for people with eye disease. Santen prides itself on its ethical principles and makes every effort to incorporate the founding philosophy of the company into all of its business activities, day after day.

Santen Incorporated, a wholly owned subsidiary of Santen Pharmaceutical Co. Ltd., opened its doors in the San Francisco Bay Area in 1993. Nestled in Northern California's Napa Valley, the U.S.-based office boasts an established team of highly experienced healthcare professionals. On average, the U.S. management team has over 20 years of industry experience with extensive knowledge and expertise based exclusively in the ophthalmic field. Responsible for the clinical development of eye care pharmaceuticals and gaining product approvals in the U.S., the Napa-based office also serves as the headquarters for Santen's business in Europe, including research and development, international product approval, sales and marketing, and distribution.

Since its inception, Santen Incorporated has enjoyed significant growth in the Napa Valley and real success entering the global pharmaceutical market. To date, the company boasts the quickest product approval on record and is poised to launch a line of ophthalmic products, each of which is uniquely positioned to be a category leader. Whether in state-of-the-art antibiotics for ocular infections or in the first treatment for the prevention of allergic conjunctivitis, each new world-class product entry contributes to Santen's growing international presence as technical leader in the ophthalmic pharmaceutical market.

Outside of its international success, what makes Santen Incorporated unique is its commitment to creating a cooperative and comfortable workplace in a peaceful community. "The concept of quality of life is an important asset that would differentiate us," states Jerry Hansen, President of Santen Incorporated. "Santen Incorporated was started from scratch, without history or baggage. As CEO, my first task was to take the company west. It all came together in Napa. The business fundamentals are extraordinary—we have a healthy respect for the strength of the work ethic here." Mr. Hansen strategically chose Northern California's Napa Valley as the site for the new company, with its proximity to world-class science and research facilities as well as to top-notch universities for recruitment efforts. This, combined with Napa's excellent physical resources and land availability, made the location ideal for the emerging company. Santen purchased 13 acres in Napa's new Gateway Business Park in 1993.

Santen's small-company approach to big business and its emphasis on providing a corporate environment that is focused on improving quality of life is illustrated by its integration into the Napa Valley. The company has given back to the community on a variety of levels. Santen Incorporated has members on both the advisory committees and boards of the Napa Valley Symphony and Napa Valley Opera House and members in the Napa County Land Trust. Santen Incorporated contributes funds to all of these organizations.

The United States headquarters of Santen in Napa's Gateway Business Park. Photo by Jana Russon.

The professional staff at Santen Incorporated foster a warm, community-oriented environment. Photo by Jana Russon.

Santen Incorporated brings a non-seasonal, technology driven industry to the Valley, providing an excellent balance to the agricultural emphasis of Napa's economy. With each international success, the company's continued growth brings with it the promise of new professional jobs and opportunities for the community. Santen is working hard to become the international leader in ophthalmic pharmaceuticals through its cutting-edge resources and technologies. But, equally as important, Santen is striving to become a valuable asset to the Napa Valley community through its dedication and commitment to quality of life and living. ॐ

Jerry Hansen, President of Santen Incorporated. Photo by Jana Russon

Pacific Union College

Pacific Union College has a distinguished national reputation for its success in providing a superior Christian education to its students. Originally founded in 1882 by Seventh Day Adventist pioneers, the College is located in Angwin at the crest of the tree-lined drive up Howell Mountain, ensconced among two thousand acres of forest, meadows, and farmland.

Offering sixty-five undergraduate major programs in a wide range of fields, the College includes students representing twenty-three states and thirty countries. PUC is primarily a residential school, and sixty-nine percent of the 1,600 students who attend Pacific Union. College's Angwin campus live in the college's residence halls. In addition, the College has two satellite campuses that bring the total number of students to over 1,900. Its beautiful surroundings make the College both a contemplative retreat and a challenging environment for its students as they immerse themselves in their studies and get ready to meet their futures.

Student achievement comes naturally at Pacific Union College: a high percentage of students continue on to graduate school after completing their undergraduate degrees. Nationally, PUC is rated among the top ten schools for male students accepted into medical school, and in the top twenty for female students. Science-related majors, including Biology, Chemistry, and Behavioral Science, are the most popular; the college's nursing program holds the highest number of degree candidates, with Biology as the second largest major.

Pacific Union College is matching the pace of current educational trends. As a college diploma becomes increasingly important for establishing a career, today's classroom is likely to contain students of all ages as many seek to complete postponed degrees. PUC's degree completion program, which offers majors in Business Management, Early Childhood Education, and Criminal Justice, allows students of nontraditional ages to attend classes once a week while balancing careers and families. With its success in bringing students with a wider range of experience into the classroom, this program is anticipated to grow exponentially to meet the demands of the community. In addition, Pacific Union College recently received a $500,000 grant to build the new Napa Valley Community Resource Center. The center will provide support facilities and programs for those in established or emerging professions that offer employment opportunities requiring advanced training.

The two thousand acres of forest, meadows, and farmland surrounding Pacific Union College create a contemplative and challenging environment for its students.

Education is no longer comprised of textbooks and chalkboards alone: today's students live in a fast-paced, demanding world and are prepared to change as it changes. Success is often determined by the ability to think actively, and this is well demonstrated by an enduring PUC motto: "Thinkers, not mere reflectors." As the College approaches its 118th anniversary, Pacific Union College's students are well equipped to meet the challenges of a new century. ♋

Pacific Union College, located in Angwin at the crest of Howell Mountain, possesses a distinguished national reputation for its success in providing a superior Christian education to its students.

St. Helena Hospital

Initially founded as the Rural Health Retreat in 1878, St. Helena Hospital has grown from a pastoral haven where patients could breathe fresh air and seek remedies drawn from nature into a full-service, nonprofit, acute-care hospital serving Napa and Lake counties.

With 192 licensed beds, as well as 36 beds for residential health enhancement, St. Helena Hospital is best known for its Cardiac Center, which is renowned for its 25-year history of innovation and excellence in cardiac diagnosis, intervention, surgery, and rehabilitation. St. Helena Hospital was the first hospital in the area to offer coronary angiograms, open-heart surgery, and coronary angioplasty. Moreover, its digital biplane cardiovascular lab was the first of its kind in the United States for adult use, and is the only one in a five-county region. More than 2,000 procedures are performed in the cardiovascular lab each year. The cardiovascular surgery team, which has more than 70 years of combined experience and has performed more than 15,000 open-heart procedures, is recognized for its high success rates and consistent patient satisfaction.

The Hospital offers a full range of services, as well as outside programs that benefit the health of the community. In addition to cardiac services, the Hospital serves as a regional center for general and minimally invasive surgery, women's health services, obstetrics, medical imaging, occupational health care, home health, mental health, sleep disorders, and pulmonary rehabilitation.

JobCare, the hospital's occupational health program, serves more than 500 area businesses and government offices through its two clinics, one located at the hospital, the other in south Napa. A "one-stop shop" for employers who want one group to manage all of their company's health care needs, JobCare offers a full range of services and a broad base of knowledge about the workers' compensation system, OSHA regulations, and effective management of work-related injuries. Through the Women's Center in downtown

St. Helena, St. Helena Hospital offers mammograms, bone density tests, and other women's health services, as well as support groups and resource materials.

Combining up-to-the-minute equipment and first-rate staff with a reassuring human touch, St. Helena Hospital has been promoting health with compassion and skill for over a century. The hospital's origins in encouraging healthy living and an innovative approach to medicine are apparent in its current mission: to create an effective environment for healing the whole person, where patients can rely on the hospital's experience and dedication to their well-being. Surrounded by forested hills overlooking the beautiful Napa Valley, the physicians and staff at St. Helena Hospital offer technologically advanced care in a serene environment that is unparalleled in the North Bay. ⚭

Forested hills and a serene natural environment promote a healing atmosphere at St. Helena Hospital.

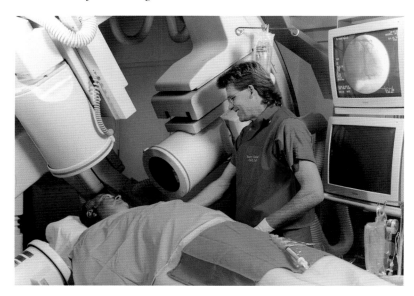

Combining up-to-the-minute technology and first-rate staff with a reassuring human touch, the hospital offers a full range of services to the region.

Napa Valley College

Napa Valley College is a two-year community college offering its students a supportive learning environment and the best in associate degree programs, college transfer courses, vocational programs, community education, and lifelong learning. The college has achieved statewide recognition for its excellent programs in such fields as viticulture, telecommunications, welding, drafting, and certification courses in nursing, psychiatric technician, respiratory therapy, and administration of justice. The reputation of the college attracts first-rate faculty, and its academic classes, from art to zoology, are among the best in the state.

The programs at Napa Valley College not only reflect the heritage of a great agricultural and wine-producing area, they also parallel the state's lead in technology development. A new Electronic Classroom, computer lab, and many classrooms provide Internet access and the latest software. The campus library is connected to the unlimited resources of online databases and offers ready access to more than one million books. A recent alliance with Cisco Systems assures that Napa Valley College students will continue to receive the finest technological training available.

Napa Valley College was founded in 1942 on a site adjacent to Napa High School. It relocated in 1965 to 180 tree-lined acres overlooking the Napa River at the southern end of the city. To serve the needs of the upper Napa Valley, a new satellite campus opened in St. Helena in 1994. As its two campuses connect the lower and upper reaches of the valley, the college looks to an exciting future with an unparalleled range of programs.

Special features at the main campus include an Olympic-sized swimming pool, a vineyard, a peaceful walking trail along the river, a model childcare facility that is part of the college's highly regarded

Napa Valley College has high academic standards and an excellent faculty. Here 1999 McPherson Distinguished Teachers Kate Benscoter, Associate Professor Respiratory Therapy, and Child and Family Studies Professor Carole Kent are pictured on the Napa campus prior to commencement. Photo by Robert Buehler.

Child and Family Studies program, English as a Second Language classes, and courses for lifelong learning through Community Education. The college's partnership with the Small Business Development Center, located in downtown Napa, provides low or no-cost workshops and counseling to assist established businesses and new entrepreneurs. The offices of Financial Aid, Special Services, Counseling, and other support services are strong factors in the success of students at Napa Valley College, which maintains a high transfer rate to four-year colleges and universities.

The Upper Valley Campus offers academic and community education as well as a vineyard and a superb culinary program unique among the 106 community colleges in California. The professional teaching kitchen on campus supports the Napa Valley Cooking School, which offers a 14 1/2-month intensive program of professional training for fine restaurants. There are also many short-term classes for culinary enthusiasts. ♨

Executive Chef George Torassa, Chef/Instructor Eric Lee, and the Napa Valley Cooking School class in the Culinary Arts building at the beautiful Upper Valley Campus in St. Helena.

Napa Valley Physicians IPA

Napa Valley Physicians (NVP), established in 1980, provides managed care administrative functions for network physician practices. These functions include contracting with health care insurance companies, administering the HMO referral and authorization program, medical care quality outcomes monitoring, nurse case management, community health education, claims processing, and joint marketing with both Valley hospitals, Queen of the Valley Hospital and St. Helena Hospital. In 1997, the physician group formed a Management Services Organizations (MSO) called Physicians Health Partnership in order to broaden its scope of managed care support services for its hospitals and to develop a vision for other aspects of healthcare improvement in the community. The Directors on the MSO Board not only include physician leaders but also hospital and community representation in order to broaden the company's scope in identifying and creatively addressing the current and future health needs of the County.

With two full-service hospitals and a network of over 140 physicians, there are broad medical resources available locally to serve the needs of the Napa County community. In addition, since nearly 20 percent of our residents are Hispanic, many of the physicians and their office staffs have addressed the bilingual requirements of

Healthcare providers in independent practices provide a refreshing alternative to clinic-style medicine.

the valley. Health Plans administered by Napa Valley Physicians IPA include PacifiCare/Secure Horizons, Health Net, California Care, Blue Shield, Aetna US Healthcare, Prudential, and 13 non-HMO Preferred Provider Plans.

NVP interacts directly with employers on several fronts. On a daily basis, our member services department answers questions and facilitates problem solving with employers and their employees. We also meet regularly with employers, along with representatives from Queen of the Valley Hospital and St. Helena Hospital and a local health insurance broker to inform employers about the HMO coverage options available to access local physicians and our excellent hospitals. Since health insurance rates are now very competitive, Napa employers, who prefer to promote local businesses and services, often find they are pleasantly surprised when they realize that they can offer a market-priced benefit plan for their employees that utilizes community resources to the fullest. The integrated system also provides health education classes that are on-going, usually free of charge, and offered up and down the Valley.

Napa Valley Physicians IPA, through its MSO, integrates physicians, hospitals, and community partners into a system that can deliver quality managed health care that meets or exceeds the expectations of patients, providers, and payors. Its guiding principles include the application of the highest standards of excellence to the delivery of health care while contributing positively to the Napa Valley community. ☙

Napa Valley Physicians works with both community hospitals to balance administration needs with the personal side of health care.

CHAPTER 8

Manufacturing & Construction

Cultured Stone Corporation

One of the largest and fastest growing companies in the Napa Valley, Cultured Stone Corporation was originally founded in Vallejo by two brothers, Garrett and Floyd Brown. The brothers, who were trained and working as plasterers, began making manufactured stone in 1962. Their first expansion into a wider market found them distributing manufactured stone to businesses in Northern and Southern California; since then, the company has enjoyed tremendous growth. Today Cultured Stone Corporation distributes its primary product line, Cultured Stone®, to customers through more than 850 dealers in North America and in over 20 countries.

Cultured Stone Corporation is the world's largest producer of manufactured stone veneer and precast stone surfaces, offering a wide range of innovative products to bring the sophisticated look of natural stone to both commercial and residential customers. The Napa-based company's portfolio of trademarks boasts an impressive variety of stone-look products with a wide range of applications. Cultured Stone®, the brand name of the company's primary product, represents the fusing of the beautiful look of natural stone with function, practicality, and ease of installation. Culture Stone® products are lightweight, accessible alternatives to full-thickness natural stone, cast in molds that are carefully created by master craftsmen and designed to mimic genuine stone in a variety of shapes, textures, and sizes. They are made from natural ingredients, including Portland cement, lightweight aggregates, and iron-oxide pigments.

Delivering the attractive look of natural stone in an extensive variety of styles, Cultured Stone® products possess many advantages that make them preferable to ordinary stone. Colors and textures are unfailingly consistent from batch to batch and year to year. Because they are lightweight, they are less cumbersome than full-thickness stone and do not require the same structural provisions as natural stone. Cultured Stone® products are durable and backed by a 50-year limited warranty. Also, they are specifically designed for smooth installation and design flexibility. Cultured Stone® products are shaped and sized to fit any space easily, and nearly the entire line of wall veneer stones features matching 90-degree corners. The functionality, quality, and the ease with which Cultured Stone®

products can be installed make them an affordable alternative to natural stone, and the preference of many builders.

Many businesses in the Napa Valley have found Cultured Stone® products ideal for bringing the look of natural stone to their construction projects; many of the beautiful homes and buildings in the valley find inspiration in natural textures and colors. One example of Cultured Stone® veneer can be seen at the new Target store in the South Napa Marketplace, which boasts an exterior custom-color application of Cultured Stone® Water Wash texture. Other projects in Napa which display the company's product offerings are the Silverado Country Club and many wineries and residential projects.

Cultured Stone® products come in a vast array of styles, colors, and textures, and have an unlimited range of applications, from commercial to residential construction. The look of stone enhances any surface— fireplaces, exterior walls, chimneys, landscaping, facades, patios, columns, or pathways: there is a Cultured Stone® product for every situation. The company's four main product lines are Cultured Stone® veneers, which come in such textures as Fieldstone, River Rock, Limestone, and Castle Stone; Cultured Brick®, which gives the look of full-thickness brick in a variety of colors; Terra Craft® Pavers and landscape products, which include stepping stones, landscape edging, and San Francisco Cobblestone® pavers; and architectural trim products such as precast window and door trim, waterables and sills, capstones and hearthstones.

Cultured Stone® Stream Stone-Summer Standard.

Cultured Stone® Water Wash texture featured at Target in the South Napa Marketplace.

Cultured Stone®
Drystack Ledgestone.

Cultured Stone® products provide the character and appeal of natural stone to homeowners looking for an affordable way to enhance and add value to their homes, to builders wishing to upgrade and differentiate their products, and to architectural and design firms who know that specifying genuine Cultured Stone® products guarantees quality.

Cultured Stone Corporation has grown from a local company into a member of the international economic community. Cultured Stone® is an Owens Corning business, a global company with over 5 billion dollars in sales and approximately 20,000 employees

worldwide. An undisputed band leader in the building products industry, Cultured Stone® is assuredly the most recognized name in manufactured stone products and precast stone architectural accessories. In the last two years, Cultured Stone Corporation has completed significant expansion at its Napa facility; the company owns over 27 acres of manufacturing facilities and employs more than 800 people. Solid in its reputation, Cultured Stone Corporation has been the industry's preeminent designer of manufactured stone since its founding almost 40 years ago and anticipates significant growth in the near future. 𝄞

Cultured Stone Corporation.

Eberlin Construction

Stunning homes nestled in the hills of Napa Valley are examples of the melange of styles found in the area and the simple joy for living that their inhabitants possess. These houses are the handiwork of Bob Eberlin of Eberlin Construction. Painstakingly crafted, they represent the fusion of diverse elements and unique character that make the Napa Valley a singular and delightful place to live.

In addition to custom homes, other Eberlin projects can be seen around the valley. The construction company built Reverie Vineyards, Diamond Creek Vineyards, Farella Park Winery, and Raymond Vineyard's new facility. Along with these projects, Eberlin has completed many smaller jobs for other vineyards, including Beaulieu Vineyards and Benessere Vineyards.

A Bay Area native, Bob Eberlin began his career as a custom home contractor in the Lake Tahoe area. Returning to the Bay Area in the late 1960s, Eberlin continued to build custom homes; during this time he met Peter Stocker, one of the principals of Pacific Union Company. A San Francisco-based development company whose properties include several San Francisco hotels and Napa Valley Gateway, Pacific Union Company also owns St. Helena's world-famous Meadowood Resort.

Eberlin was selected by Stocker to remodel the prestigious club; however, during construction a fire broke out and decimated the resort. After the catastrophe, Stocker sought the help of architect Kirk Hillman. Hillman went to the design table and returned with

Meadowood Resort, the exclusive St. Helena club celebrated for its exceptional dining and refined accommodations, is one example of Eberlin's craftsmanship on display in the Napa Valley.

the plans for the newly designed Meadowood, and Eberlin went to work building the sumptuous resort that visitors see today. Once Eberlin was settled in St. Helena working on the new Meadowood, he fell in love with the valley, relocated permanently, and continued building custom homes and taking on other projects in the area.

Though they build dreams, Eberlin Construction has its feet planted firmly on the ground. "We have a style of doing business that is a little bit different," says Kay Doughty, project manager for Eberlin Construction. "We don't have a fancy office or other such trappings. While we're quality oriented, we're a no frills operation.

"I also think that we're a little unique in that most of the guys who work for us have worked for us for many years. In construction you tend to have tremendous turnover: you see new faces on crews all the time," says Doughty. However, the comfortable, informal atmosphere at Eberlin Construction encourages a sense of family that has created a strong bond among the company's employees. "Of the people who work on our jobs, most all of them have been with us for eight or ten years and some much longer than that. There's a lot of continuity in the crew. Everybody really knows each other well, and I think the clients appreciate that."

Eberlin Construction brings the expertise necessary to make custom home clients' dreams a reality.

*Renovations are breathing
new life into Napa's
downtown area.*

CHAPTER 9

Business &
Finance

Napa Chamber of Commerce

As the membership organization for business, we promote our community's economic vitality and quality of life through leadership development, advocacy, facilitation, and education. This is the mission statement of the Napa Chamber of Commerce.

An organization at the forefront of contemporary Napa's thriving economy, the Napa Chamber of Commerce grew from the elemental needs of an isolated community of 3,000 in 1889. Napa was facing several particularly urgent concerns: few job opportunities; lack of basic necessities; warped, wooden sidewalks; and roads that ranged from dusty to muddy in summer heat and winter rain. On September 30, 1889, postmaster and owner of the Napa Register George M. Francis called a public meeting at the courthouse to address the town's most important issues. Supported by the 80 citizens who met that day, the Napa Improvement Society was created, with local merchant E. D. Beard elected as president. Over the next 15 years the membership became convinced that they could be most effective by concentrating on economic improvements; they renamed themselves the Napa Board of Trade in 1896 and ultimately the Napa Chamber of Commerce on January 25, 1904.

One thing that hasn't changed in more than 110 years is the sense of community, not only among Chamber members but also within the larger context of the valley environment. In many ways, Napa Improvement Society could still serve as a fair descriptor of the Chamber. Chamber members work alongside city and county

A gathering of past presidents of the Napa Chamber of Commerce, representing almost 20 years of service to the business community. Photo by Margretha Lane.

government leaders to support the area's economic interests, although the Chamber is funded entirely by its own activities and receives no government funding. The Chamber is led by a volunteer board of 30 men and women who set policy, communicate with the membership to find out what the issues are, and decide upon the Chamber's programs; the staff are the ones who day to day implement those policies and programs.

Kate King, Executive Director of the Napa Chamber of Commerce since June 1999, is very proud of the Chamber's accomplishments and the dedication of its staff and volunteers. Chamber staff includes LuAnn McClure, Database Manager; T.F. "Rick" Wells, Jr., Membership Manager; Sue Fisher, Receptionist; Karen Calhoun, Publications/Events; and Stephanie Murray, Administrative Assistant.

The volunteer team members of the Chamber Ambassadors are kept busy welcoming and visiting businesses throughout the valley. Each year the Chamber sponsors a golf tournament to benefit such programs as the Napa Police Department's graffiti control program. Other activities of the Chamber range from keeping members informed about important legislative issues to forums, seminars, and regular mixers where members and nonmembers network and socialize. With the radio station KVON as co-sponsor, the Chamber selects a Citizen of the Year, to pay tribute to men and women who give extraordinary volunteer service to the community. Annual Business Showcases and Economic Summits keep everyone informed on the latest business trends in Napa.

With five years of experience as a chamber CEO, Kate King is very realistic and forthright about the job ahead. Because of the large number of regulations in California it is particularly challenging for businesses to be competitive and to do well in the state. "We're focused on really creating the kind of environment that makes businesses thrive; we branch out and look at the community itself to see what we can do to help keep the quality of life here so that it's a place where businesses want to stay," says King.

"Whether you're an industrial park in the south county or a retailer downtown or a vineyard up north, there's a place in the Chamber for you and your input is important"—Kate King, CEO, Napa Chamber of Commerce. Aerial photo by Ron Ruiz.

"We probably have a higher percentage of people who work and live in the same area as opposed to metropolitan areas where they live in the suburbs or somewhere far away. It makes for a different atmosphere, a different commitment. The people in Napa are extremely committed to their community and to maintaining a really high quality of life. Yet because they are business people, they have the acumen to realize there has to be an infusion of new dollars and new industry—and new and innovative ways of doing business—in order to stay competitive.

"There's a global market now. I have heard from people elsewhere who do business with people in Napa that, for being such a quaint, historical, and lovely place, we have some of the most sophisticated business people they've ever seen, including our agricultural community."

Another trait of Napa's Chamber is the diversity of its membership. Says King, "We have everything literally from the Tupperware lady to Dey Laboratories, our largest private employer. There's a myriad of needs, so we have everything from an arts and culture committee to a business committee to a job resources committee to a professional services committee. We have all these different entities to try to address their needs."

The Napa Chamber's sphere of influence extends beyond the boundaries of the city to members all throughout the valley; it cooperates and maintains collaborative rela-

tionships with other chambers as well, through an All Chambers group. King foresees a growing opportunity for the chambers to work together on such regional issues as water and growth.

Meanwhile, what's ahead for the Napa Chamber is an even deeper commitment to its membership and Napa's business community. Says King, "We want it to be very inclusionary. Whether you're an industrial park in the south county or a retailer downtown or a vineyard up north, there's a place in the Chamber for you and your input is important." ⚭

City of Napa

Napa is a riverfront community of 70,000 people and has a rich history as well as a dazzling future. Located in one of the world's most beautiful valleys, Napa is committed to preserving its prized quality of family life as it continues to build upon its strong and sophisticated economy. Through the efforts of community volunteers and business leaders, Napa is poised to flower into a magnificent center for viticulture, fine cuisine, music, and the arts.

Napa traces its beginnings as a city to John Grigsby and Nathan Coombs, two men involved in the Bear Flag Revolt of June 1846 in Sonoma. The following year Grigsby and Coombs bartered their carpentry skills in exchange for riverfront land owned by Bear Flag sympathizer and former Mexican soldier Nicolas Higuera. The new townsite was surveyed, mapped, and dubbed Napa City, soon after renamed Napa.

The City of Napa is the seat of government in Napa County and was officially incorporated as a city on March 23, 1872. Napa operates under the Council/Manager form of government; the Mayor and the four members of the City Council hold regular meetings that are well attended by the community. The Council appoints the City Manager, City Clerk, and City Attorney; all other city employees are appointed by the City Manager, a busy hands-on position that oversees the departments of Community Resources, Economic Development/Redevelopment, Finance, Fire, Housing, Planning, Police, and Public Works.

City Manager Pat Thompson has remarked that you can understand a lot about Napa when you consider its attitude toward managed growth. As defined in the vision plan of Napa's Economic Strategic Plan, the city ". . . seeks to create a world-class city while preserving the small-scale charm and rich cultural heritage of Napa, complete with widespread scenic vistas and thriving family-oriented neighborhoods that are safe and secure."

"The wine industry, tourism industry, and the growing interest in high tech businesses moving to the airport area have maintained Napa's vital economy," according to Cassandra Walker, redevelopment director. "Even with its rural charm, Napa boasts a very sophisticated

corporate park, which has such top names as Dey Laboratories in the biotechnology field, Pan Am Sat in international telecommunications, and Quantum Information Systems."

Within the next few years, Napa will see the fruition of plans for its "Living River." The Napa River was the social and economic heart of the community in the 1800s and will be again in the 2000s. A crucial $180 million flood control measure was passed in 1998 by voters from every constituency in the valley and will be completed in seven to nine years; the unparalleled cooperation county residents demonstrated on this issue has resulted in new energy for downtown Napa, "to broaden it," as Thompson says, "from primarily a commercial center to a living, enjoyable environment. The focus will be pedestrian friendly, with new bridges including promenades that will allow people to walk from downtown to the American Center for Wine, Food and the Arts, the Expo Conference Center, the Hatt Marketplace, and along Main Street with its burgeoning nightlife and quality dining.

"We realize that people from all over the world want to come to Napa and to Napa Valley. Napa is going to be developing more of its central core into a world-class destination, a sophisticated environment that will be attractive to people who are traveling here from other countries. We are building upon our relationships within the wine country and at the same time preserving for our own citizens that feeling

A view of the tranquil Napa River as seen from Veteran's Park next to the bustling downtown businesses of the City of Napa. Photo by Gene Piscia.

The splendidly restored Opera House (pictured) in downtown Napa joins the Jarvis Conservatory and the American Center for Wine, Food, and the Arts as cornerstones of the performing arts community. Photo by Gene Piscia.

Seeking to complement rather than compete with the cultural character of other areas in the valley, Napa has chosen as its niche entertainment and the arts. The Jarvis Conservatory, an early investor in the downtown cultural renaissance, offers the community the rich and rare traditions of Spanish opera, Zarzuela, and baroque dance. Other important contributors, present and future, are the American Center for Wine, Food and the Arts, the Oxbow School for the Visual Arts, the Opera House, the artists' village in the Tannery, and the Napa Symphony, which holds outdoor concerts on downtown's Third Street Bridge. Because of the size of the community, Napa is able to host some of the valley's larger events, such as the Wine and Crafts Fair, Fourth of July Jazz Festival, and the Napa Valley Marathon.

For Mayor Ed Henderson, what is most exciting about Napa today is that "the town is abuzz with citizens and business owners talking about the potential for our community not only today, but for our children and grandchildren. . . . Now we must work to make the future really happen. I have always believed that each of us is the artist of our lives. Together, we can become the artists of the valley. What a magnificent challenge!" ☙

of being able to stay in our own community and enjoy the quiet and the peaceful vistas."

Napa has always been a great place for families to raise their children. The city's excellent schools, relaxed, kid-friendly neighborhoods, and plentiful parks are some of its most treasured features. Remarks Thompson, "One of the unique things is that the Napa community can celebrate something as famous as the World Cup bicycle races and at the same time enjoy just as much a cross-town high school football game, which probably generates as many, if not more, spectators."

CHAPTER 10

Transportation &
Public Service

Napa Garbage Service/Napa Valley Disposal Service

Ten years after the Great Earthquake of 1906 precipitated his relocation from San Francisco, Archangelo Bacigalupi came to Napa looking for a quiet place to raise his family and maintain his livelihood hauling away discards from homes and businesses. Over eight decades later, the Bacigalupi family remains in the same thriving occupation. William A. Bacigalupi, grandson of the founder, still puts in hours at the plant; William's stepson Greg Kelley, a fifth-generation Napan, is the busy general manager.

The business is a study in contrasts. Historically a rough and dirty line of work, trash disposal has necessarily become a highly technical business. From the modern company offices in south Napa County, Greg Kelley oversees a network of 70 employees and a fleet of 55 trucks, a long way from the early days when the Bacigalupi family had one wagon and two horses to serve their customers.

The family has been a part of Napa history as long as people living in the valley can remember. Archangelo started as an independent operator with one horse-drawn cart, then in 1920 entered into a more lucrative partnership with three others in the area to form the entity Napa City Garbage.

Garbage collecting of decades ago was different in many ways from that of today. As a form of erosion control, trash and garbage were burned and then turned out on the banks of the Napa River near the Oxbow until 1923. Trash consisted of scraps of food, some wood, even less paper, but a lot of ashes, since families would generally burn

as much of their rubbish as they could. Chemical pollutants were seldom among the trash of yesterday, and fish freshly caught from the adjacent river were superb, say Napa old-timers.

The work was hard for both the family and their horses. At three in the morning the family got up, fed the horses and put on their tack, then drove into the city. On icy mornings the horses couldn't manage the steep ascent on the old wooden Third Street bridge, so the men covered their horses' hooves with cloth sacks to keep them from slipping. The men first picked up discarded packing crates from the town businesses and at five swept the cobblestone streets around the courthouse. They continued along the rest of their route until noon, filling the carts with rubbish to take to the dump and burn. Glass, tin, and anything that still had use left in it was recycled. Old clothing and rags were 100 percent cotton and could readily be sold, processed, and reused. Food scraps were sometimes salvageable as feed for the chickens and pigs the Bacigalupis and their partners raised to support their families. The work didn't end when the cart pulled into the drive at home: the horses needed tending; wet sacks had to be spread on the wagon wheels to keep the spokes taut; the wooden flour barrels used for collecting needed to be filled with water to keep them watertight.

The ensuing years brought growth and progress to Napa, and with more prosperity, more trash to haul away. In 1923, the dumping grounds were moved out of town to an old rock quarry east of Tulocay Cemetery. In 1930, the company bought its first truck, a Model A, to augment its small fleet of two horse-drawn carts; in

A rare 1910 photograph of the founding Baciagalupi family, their two horses, and hauling cart.

Nine-year-old William Bacigalupi in 1947 sits atop one of the company's two trucks at the old headquarters at Clay and Juarez Strets.

1935, a second truck was added and the horses were given a well-earned retirement. The war years brought even more changes to the valley due to the activity of the shipyards at nearby Mare Island.

In 1989, the company began five years of researching recycling operations throughout the state and then incorporated the best processes into its new Napa facilities in 1994. Today, Napa Garbage Service is making great strides environmentally and expects to meet the state's Year 2000 goal of recycling 50 percent of collected solid waste. The yard waste program annually produces over 40,000 tons of

Napa's cleaner and safer automated collecting systems benefit both customers and workers.

true organic compost which is certified by the California Compost Quality Council and marketed to local vineyards and soil producers. Napa's cleaner and safer automated collecting systems benefit both customers and workers and keep labor costs down. Responding to city and community needs, the company is expanding into construction and demolition recycling, thus providing raw materials for electrical power and roadways and saving tons of materials from winding up in landfills. All recycled cardboard is baled and most goes to domestic mills; newspapers go to mills in Santa Clara; aluminum goes to Kaiser

and Alcoa; and glass bottles are crushed, remanufactured, and back on shelves within 28 days.

The company supplies landscaping materials to local schools and offers educational programs and field trips to its recycling facilities to school children, environmental clubs, and the Boy Scouts. Especially rewarding is the work program the company provides through Napa Valley Support Services in which developmentally challenged adults work four-hour shifts safely sorting recyclable paper and cardboard. The clients take pride in earning their wages and contributing a valuable service to the community.

William A. Bacigalupi speaks with both pride and affection of the company his grandfather began. Even though Napa Garbage Service is now part of the world's largest waste collector, Waste Management, the founding family is still managing the day-to-day business. By keeping its priorities attuned to local needs, the company has grown from a one-horse show into an efficient multi-million-dollar operation. ꩜

Community recycling conserves natural resources and produces over 40,000 tons of true organic compost.

Napa County Transportation Planning Agency (NCTPA)

One of the newest and most active agencies in the valley is the Napa County Transportation Planning Agency. Formed in June 1998, NCTPA is the planning and policy-making authority for countywide transportation issues, including highways, streets and roads, transit and paratransit, as well as bicycle and pedestrian improvements.

In the last few years, local growth and land-use issues have had an increasingly important impact on planning for area transit needs. The formation of NCTPA is an indication that public officials understand the critical role mobility plays in making a community accessible to its residents and visitors. In forming NCTPA, three agencies were restructured: the Napa County Congestion Management Agency, the city of Napa fixed-route system of public transit (the V.I.N.E.—"Valley Intracity Neighborhood Express"—and Napa Valley Transit), and the county's VanGo system for seniors and the disabled. The NCTPA Board is composed of eight voting members—two members from the Napa County Board of Supervisors, two council members from the City of Napa, and one council member each from the cities of Calistoga, St. Helena and American Canyon, and the town of Yountville—plus one nonvoting member from the Elderly and Disabled Advisory Committee.

Since public transit doesn't simply stop at jurisdictional borders, the agency operates with considerable cooperation and coordination to assure that public transportation works as seamlessly as possible for the people who rely upon it. Napa Valley Transit buses travel to Calistoga and upvalley attractions, connect with V.I.N.E. buses throughout the city of Napa, link with Vallejo Transit and BARTlink buses, and meet incoming and outgoing BAYLINK ferries in Vallejo. Transfers between systems are timed carefully to minimize waiting between connections.

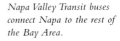

Napa Valley Transit buses connect Napa to the rest of the Bay Area.

All V.I.N.E. and Napa Valley Transit buses are equipped with easy-to-use bike racks. There are special fares for students, children, and disabled persons. Free tape-recorded schedules and information cassettes are available for the blind and vision impaired.

NCTPA has been busy formulating a strategic transportation plan to ensure the valley's transit system evolves efficiently and effectively. NCTPA's highest priority is improving mobility for county residents as well as making transit easier for visitors to use while minimizing congestion. Other priorities are minimizing duplication of transit services, making sure each jurisdiction receives its fair share of federal and state funding for road, highway, and public transit projects, and improving air quality.

In June 2000, NCTPA is scheduled to receive its first alternative-fuel buses. One of the most immediate and anticipated goals is to relocate the outgrown Pearl Street terminal in Napa to a more efficient location. A new terminal could blend with new riverfront development, retail spaces, a parking garage, and innovative childcare facilities. ✎

Napa Valley Transit gets you there!

Napa Enterprise Index

Index